Software Defined Networking (SDN): Anatomy of OpenFlow

Doug Marschke, Jeff Doyle and Pete Moyer

ISBN: 978-1-4834-2723-2 (sc)
ISBN: 978-1-4834-2724-9 (e)

Because of the dynamic nature of the Internet, any web addresses or links contained in this book may have changed since publication and may no longer be valid. The views expressed in this work are solely those of the author and do not necessarily reflect the views of the publisher, and the publisher hereby disclaims any responsibility for them.

Any people depicted in stock imagery provided by Thinkstock are models, and such images are being used for illustrative purposes only. Certain stock imagery © Thinkstock.

Lulu Publishing Services rev. date: 3/25/2015

Contents

Preface

Software Defined Networking, just a few short years ago, was mostly speculation. Sure there were academics doing research with it, and there were some hyper-scale networks like Google and Amazon using it. But those places were crawling with programmers and developers. Most people running normal sized networks viewed it with curiosity, but not much else. They certainly didn't have the resources to build SDN architectures in-house. And many – perhaps even one or more authors of this book – scoffed at the idea that SDN would turn the networking world on its head.

What a difference a few years make. Almost every vendor now has an SDN story. New vendors are popping up everywhere with SDN products. Solutions are being deployed and new use cases are presented regularly. You can find an SDN conference somewhere in the world every few weeks, and it's a central topic of major industry conferences from Cisco Live and VMWorld to Interop and Cloud Expo. Network engineers are beginning to reassess the skill sets they will need over the next ten years or so.

SDN is quickly proving to be every bit as disruptive as it was predicted to be.

Why Did We Write This Book?

For all the attention SDN is getting, it remains a vague concept for many people. Products are still young, and standards are still being developed. All three of the authors have had the experience of having to define SDN to our customers before being able to discuss it with them.

This book is the first in a planned series on SDN, intended to help you navigate the many protocols and technologies comprising the SDN family of architectures. Future topics will cover Network Function Virtualization, orchestration, and SDN in the WAN.

Why Start with OpenFlow?

More than a few of our friends in the industry, when we've said we're writing a book on OpenFlow, have said, "Really? Why OpenFlow? Isn't it teetering on obsolescence?"

Well, no it isn't. Some vendors have gone other directions with their controller-to-switch protocols. And OpenFlow is evolving from its original mission of only building flow tables in switches to now specifying configurations, security, and policy. But there is still wide interest in and support for the protocol, and the Working Groups establishing OpenFlow standards are among the most well established in the industry. It will be around for a long time.

So OpenFlow, as a proven and open SDN protocol sitting in the middle of all the action between controllers and switches, is an excellent subject for beginning a study of SDN architectures.

Is This Book for You?

You're reading this preface, so you obviously are curious enough about SDN to have picked up or downloaded the book. It is our opinion that yes, that's enough to say this book is for you. We've organized the book so that you can skim it for an introduction to SDN and a quick overview of how SDN uses OpenFlow as a foundation protocol, or you can use the book for a deep dive into the protocol and its use.

We've written the book with data center architects, engineers, troubleshooters, and students in mind. We hope you get as much out of reading it as we got out of writing it.

Schedule of the Book Series

As you know if you are following or involved in SDN, things are changing at an accelerated pace. Innovation cannot be held back! Volume I provides the needed background and baseline of SDN, for which Volume II expands on with NFV and other emerging technologies. Some of the use cases in Volume I might be old news but they provide the proper background and basis for understanding how things are rapidly evolving as SDN moves forward.

Volume II will be published in 2015 and Volume III will be published in late 2015 or early 2016.

Author: Jeff Doyle

Specializing in IP routing protocols, SDN, data center fabrics, MPLS, and IPv6, Jeff Doyle has designed or assisted in the design of large-scale IP service provider networks in 26 countries over 6 continents. He worked with early IPv6 adopters in Japan, China, and South Korea, and now advises service providers, government agencies, military contractors, equipment manufacturers, and large enterprises on best-practice IPv6 deployment.

Jeff is the author of *CCIE Professional Development: Routing TCP/IP*, Volumes I and II; *OSPF and IS-IS: Choosing an IGP for Large-Scale Networks*; and is an editor and contributing author of *Juniper Networks Routers: The Complete Reference*. He also writes blogs for both Network World and for Network Computing. Jeff is one of the founders of the Rocky Mountain IPv6 Task Force and is an IPv6 Forum Fellow.

Author: Doug Marschke

Doug Marschke is an engineering graduate from the University of Michigan and founder of SDN Essentials. He is a writer of various Juniper certification exams and co-writer of the JNCIE Enterprise Exam. He has also authored the *JUNOS Enterprise Routing* book, and *JUNOS Enterprise Switching*.

Doug currently spends his time working with both service providers and enterprises to optimize their IP networks for better performance, cost and reliability. He also flies around the word and back sharing his knowledge in a variety of training classes and seminars with topics ranging from troubleshooting, design and certification preparation. In Doug's free time he is an entrepreneur of sorts as he owns two restaurants in San Francisco, Taco Shop at Underdogs and Tacko. He also has dabbled into the world of film with his production company, Funny How Films.

Author: Pete Moyer

Pete Moyer is an old timer IP/MPLS consulting engineer who has turned his focus toward SDN in recent years. He is currently employed by Brocade and has multi-vendor experience in IP networking; he earned the first awarded JNCIE in the early 2000's and he earned his CCIE in the late 1990's. He was previously with Juniper for approximately 10 years. He is a co-author and technical editor of several IP networking books. His current focus is on large-scale data center and service provider networks, including the Research & Education Network (REN) market. He holds a BS, CMIS from the University of Maryland.

Technical Editor:

Chris Jones is an SDN Engineer with SDN Essentials, certified with Juniper as JNCIE-ENT #272, and with Cisco Systems as CCIE #25655 (R&S). He has over a decade of industry experience with both Cisco and Juniper products and solutions, designing and building networks for both small and large enterprises as well as for major service providers. Chris is the author of the Proteus Networks *JNCIE-ENT Preparation Workbook*, as well as the Juniper Networks Day One book *Junos for IOS Engineers*.

Graphics Editor:

Gregg Martin currently leads Solutions Arcitecture for Fishnet Security. Gregg has over 18 years of experience in Information Technology, and over 15 years of experience in Enterprise Networking. Prior to joining Fishnet Security, Gregg was with PricewaterhouseCoopers ("PwC") for 10 years and worked as a Network Engineer and Network Architect, responsible for the architecture of all network and security technologies for the entire firm. Gregg's delivered the built out of numerous data centers and well versed in the design, implementation, and operations of network and security technologies for data centers. In addition, Gregg has conducted audits and reviews of data of several well known industry data centers

Acknowledgements:

Jeff would like to thank his wife Sara for her immense patience and encouragement over many years of writing projects, extended travel, and the general insanity that comes with being in the networking industry. He would also like to thank his two co-authors not only for the things he has learned from them, but for many, many years of friendship. Doug and Pete are two of the best people I know.

Pete would like to thank his fantastic family for their support while he worked long hours and late nights co-authoring this book: Kathy, Jazmin, Kristin and Lorin. And he can't resist a shout-out to his most lovable mother, Mrs. Moyer (Sakugawa).

Doug would like to thank Pete and Jeff for stepping up and making this book happen despite my best efforts to slow things down. I would also like to thank every person around me, who dealt with my stress level while trying to get this book done, and want to proactively thank them all as we move onto volume 2. Lastly, I would like to thank Trish, Jordan and Ferb for their lasting support as I typed away in my work cave each evening.

Introduction

Software Defined Networking (SDN) has been a wildly successful buzzword (or perhaps, buzz acronym?). Every networking vendor has to have a Software Defined Networking story. Rarely does a marketing brief get out the door these days without "SDN" somewhere in the text. Judging from the trade journals you might think that little else is happening in the networking world except clouds and SDN.

The term is so popular that it has spawned a litter of similar terms yapping around our ankles. Software Defined Data Center. Software Defined Storage. Software Defined Security. Software Defined Application Delivery. Network Function Virtualization (software defined, of course).

All the industry hype leaves CIOs and CTOs scratching their heads over what SDN really is, and what it means for their business. I know, roughly, that SDN involves the separation of the control plane from the data plane. I know it involves network programmability. I know it abstracts the data plane, but what does that actually mean? Is OpenFlow the same thing as SDN? What's the difference between SDN and Network Functions Virtualization (NFV)? Can I gracefully integrate SDN into my existing systems, or when they call it a "disruptive technology" do they mean *I'm* the one that can expect the disruptions?

Most important of all, what is the business case for SDN?

Although this book is about OpenFlow, it's important to first understand SDN and OpenFlow's role in the SDN architecture. This chapter addresses basic concepts – and answers some basic questions – to set the stage for a proper discussion of OpenFlow.

What is SDN?

Let's start with two definitions, one very specific and one much more generalized. They represent the two endpoints of the wide range of definitions you'll encounter in the industry.

Definition 1:
SDN is an L2/L3 architecture in which a centralized controller controls the forwarding behavior of a set of distributed switches.

Definition 2:
SDN is a conceptual framework in which networks are treated as abstractions and are controlled programmatically, with minimal direct "touch" of individual network components.

Those two definitions hardly appear to be describing the same thing. But they might be. You'll frequently hear SDN defined with some version of Definition #1, but that's just a subset of the much more accurate Definition #2.

We'll start with the first definition, and see how that leads us to the second definition.

Control Planes and Data Planes

The overall SDN architecture represents an evolutionary continuum that has been happening since the early days of networking. Conceptually, there had long been a functional separation between the management, data, and forwarding planes in switches – particularly Layer 3 switches (routers).

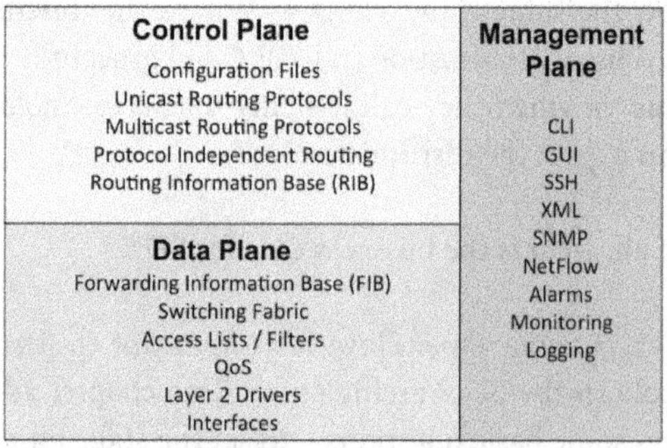

Control Plane	Management Plane
Configuration Files	
Unicast Routing Protocols	
Multicast Routing Protocols	CLI
Protocol Independent Routing	GUI
Routing Information Base (RIB)	SSH
	XML
Data Plane	SNMP
Forwarding Information Base (FIB)	NetFlow
Switching Fabric	Alarms
Access Lists / Filters	Monitoring
QoS	Logging
Layer 2 Drivers	
Interfaces	

Figure 1.1: Operational Planes of a Router

At a very simple level, the functional planes are classified as follows:

- The **Management** plane provides operational access and monitoring. The Command Line Interface (CLI) and such functions as Simple Network Management Protocol (SNMP), syslog, and NetFlow reside here.

- The **Data** or **Forwarding** plane consists of the interfaces or ports that receive and transmit Protocol Data Units (PDUs), a switching fabric, and the information necessary to guide the correct switching of PDUs between interfaces. For example, in a router the information is contained in a Forwarding Information Base (FIB) that specifies what interface a packet with a given destination address should be switched to, and the Layer 2 encapsulation information for that outgoing interface. An Ethernet switch has a table that maps MAC addresses to ports.

- The **Control** plane is responsible for giving the data plane the information it needs to correctly switch (that is, forward) PDUs. A router's control plane runs some routing protocol such as OSPF, IS-IS, or BGP; arbitrates the information it learns about IP destinations and selects preferred forwarding interfaces; and updates the FIB in the Forwarding plane.

The control plane is considered the "intelligence" in the network because it makes all the important decisions about PDU forwarding such as optimal path to a given destination, loop avoidance, flow classification, failure recovery, and traffic engineering. The data plane is concerned only with switching PDUs from incoming ports to destination ports as quickly and efficiently as it can. It makes no real decisions about how or where to switch the PDUs.

Switch? Router?

We've become accustomed to thinking of a switch" as a Layer 2 device: A frame relay switch, an ATM switch, or, if we just say "switch" by itself, it's usually understood that we mean an Ethernet switch.

When we say "router," we understand that to be an entity that makes forwarding decisions based on Layer 3 addresses and header fields rather than Layer 2 addresses and header fields. In an Ethernet context, a router communicates between broadcast domains. In a topological context, a router might connect LANs across a WAN.

And then there are so-called "Layer 3 switches." Are those Ethernet switches with a built-in router? Or are they routers with built-in Ethernet switching and lots of Ethernet ports?

Blurring the line further, load balancers switch at Layer 4 or Layer 7.

All of this confusion in terminology arises from a combination of marketing trying to differentiate products along sales verticals and engineers trying to keep products classified according to their roles in a network.

In reality they're all switches. The differentiation is just *what* they switch. An entity could be switching PDUs from incoming to outgoing ports based solely on MAC addresses or DLCIs or MPLS labels. Or it could be switching based on IP addresses. Throw QoS, microflows, or application flows into the mix, and it could be switching based on some combination of Layer 2, 3, 4, and even Layer 7 information.

OpenFlow rightly ducks all this confusion and just uses the term "switch," regardless of what kind of data unit the device is switching.

The late 1990s saw the advent of high-end routers that implemented the control and data planes in separate hardware within a chassis. Whether the manufacturer called the independent control plane a Route Processor, a Supervisor Module, a Routing Engine, or something else (marketing again), the advantages were the same: heavy loads on the control plane in times of network instability did not affect performance of the data plane, and heavy traffic loads in the data plane did not affect performance of the control plane. In fact the data plane could, at least for short periods, run "headless" – that is, with the control plane disengaged – leading to High Availability (HA) features such as Non-Stop Forwarding (NSF) and In-Service Software Upgrades (ISSU).[1]

MPLS brought another change in how the data and control planes interrelated. The "intelligence" of the network moved to the edge, where MPLS Provider Edge (PE) routers made the best-path decisions and the Provider (P) routers in the core concerned themselves mainly with just switching packets. However, MPLS P routers still had their own control planes that, while not as deterministic as the control planes in the PEs, still played a role in the router's operation.

---

[1] Old-time telephony engineers tend to snicker when we network types talk about control and data plane separation as if it was some brilliant innovation of the 1990s. They had been doing the same thing for decades.

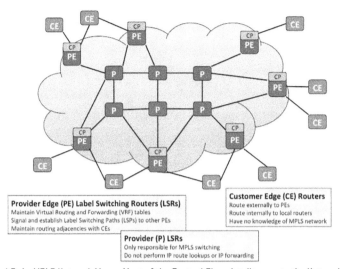

Provider Edge (PE) Label Switching Routers (LSRs)	Customer Edge (CE) Routers
Maintain Virtual Routing and Forwarding (VRF) tables	Route externally to PEs
Signal and establish Label Switching Paths (LSPs) to other PEs	Route internally to local routers
Maintain routing adjacencies with CEs	Have no knowledge of MPLS network

Provider (P) LSRs
Only responsible for MPLS switching
Do not perform IP route lookups or IP forwarding

Figure 1.2: An MPLS Network Moves Most of the Control Plane Intelligence to the Network Edge.

MPLS networks shifted the way we think of control planes in an IP network. We had spent many years optimizing the control plane to work in distributed topologies. Every router had its own control, but they could not make forwarding decisions independently. Using routing protocols, they all had to agree about what constitutes a best path to each known destination. Key challenges were the time it took for each control to converge on the same information about the network, the time and processing required to calculate reliable best paths, and the avoidance of both steady-state and transient loops. MPLS, by pushing most of the control plane responsibilities to the edge of the network, reduced the challenges of distributed control.

Together, these two trends – a control plane implemented as a separate hardware entity and pushing the control plane to the edge of the network – led to the basic SDN architecture[2] depicted in Figure 1.3. In this architecture, the "brains" of the network are centralized into a controller updating the forwarding information to all of the switches in the network.

---

[2] A "Software Defined Network" does not, by definition, require a centralized controller. The term only implies a programmable network. But a centralized controller, interfacing southbound to the Forwarding plane and northbound to some kind of programming interface, is the most logical supporting architecture for SDN.

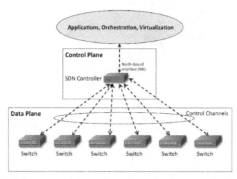

Figure 1.3: A Basic SDN Architecture: A Centralized Control Plane Controls a Distributed Data Plane.

A centralized controller solves a number of problems inherent to distributed control planes:

- Response to link or node failures should be much faster, because information about the failure does not have to be communicated through multiple nodes.
- Loop avoidance should be simpler because the controller has a "complete picture" of the network.
- Most important to the idea of programmable networks, the controller represents a single interface between the data plane and the users or applications orchestrating the forwarding.

Of course, a centralized controller introduces a different set of concerns:

- A single controller represents a single point of failure for the entire network. So there must be a means of multihoming to redundant, synchronized controllers.
- A centralized controller is an inviting attack target. If you can compromise the controller, you own the network.
- FIB updates from the controller to the switch could cause temporarily inconsistent forwarding, and hence microloops. Of course this same concern exists for individual chassis with separate control and forwarding hardware, but geographic distance can exacerbate the problem.

One of the most oft-cited advantages of an architecture like the one in Figure 1.3 – if not the most cited – is that an operator can very quickly roll out network changes (the buzzword is "network agility"). The change is specified to the controller, which determines the forwarding instructions necessary to implement the change, and the controller then sends the forwarding instructions to the switches making up the network. The operator does not have to configure each switch individually, and does not have to know the operating system command set of every vendor's switch in the network.

What is OpenFlow?

It's next to impossible for a controller to know the operating system command set for every switch in the network, too. Even from a single vendor there can be multiple operating systems, each with a command syntax that varies from a little to a lot. Take, for example, Cisco Systems. In a large network, even if it is all-Cisco, you might be running IOS, IOS-XR, CAT-OS, and NX-OS, all of which support different capabilities and use slightly different syntaxes. Add to that a mix of software releases for each, and the variation in capabilities becomes even more complicated. And the fact is that when you look at all the switching devices in your network – not just Ethernet switches and routers but also firewalls, load balancers, web accelerators, address translators, WAN optimizers, tunnel servers, Intrusion Detection System / Intrusion Prevention System (IDS/IPS), and so on – it's unlikely that they are all coming from a single vendor.

So there must be an open communications standard between the controller and the switch, and that's where OpenFlow comes in. OpenFlow defines:

- A set of flow instructions that comprise the forwarding behavior of the switch
- A set of messages that the switch can send to the controller to inform the controller of changes that might effect forwarding
- A format for containing the instructions and messages
- A protocol for sending and receiving the messages between the controller and the switch

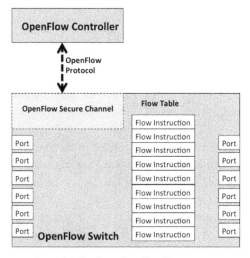

Figure 1.4: The Basic OpenFlow Components

At a high level, then, OpenFlow consists of the following components:

- The controller
- The OpenFlow interface in the switch
- A secure channel between the controller and the switch
- A flow table, which holds the flow instructions

These are only the most basic components. Chapter 3 is a detailed exploration of OpenFlow's sub-components, processes, and message structures, but this high-level definition is sufficient for you to understand the role OpenFlow plays in an SDN architecture. Simply put:

OpenFlow is a communications protocol running between the control plane and the data plane, which allows the control plane to specify the forwarding behavior of the data plane.

It's important to understand not only what OpenFlow is, but also what it is not.

OpenFlow does not specify a controller or a switch. It only specifies a means of communicating between the two, and what is communicated.

OpenFlow does not run anywhere *except* between the control plane and the data plane. It has a distinct place in an SDN architecture.

OpenFlow is not used to create networks or network elements. It's used only to control data plane forwarding behavior.

OpenFlow is not the only means by which the control plane and the data plane can communicate. Alternatives to OpenFlow include NETCONF, Extensible Message and Presence Protocol (XMPP), BGP, Open vSwitch Database Management Protocol (OVSDB), and Cisco's onePK.

Like OpenFlow, many of its alternatives are open standards – which enable multivendor implementations and an Application Programming Interface (API) for development and innovation. But OpenFlow has a leg up on other solutions because of the wide range of vendor support and its strong development community. OpenFlow also stands apart from most of its alternatives in that it pushes forwarding instructions directly into the FIB or TCAM of the switch hardware, whereas most of the alternatives talk to an operating system on the local node. This leads to an ongoing debate about whether the alternatives defeat the purpose of removing the control plane from individual nodes, or whether some level of control plane and operating system will always reside on individual nodes, SDN or no SDN.

A Simple SDN Architecture

So far we've answered the "what" of SDN and OpenFlow; we also need to answer the "why." Without a compelling business case, the cleverest of technical solutions will come to a lonely end.

An appreciation of SDN begins with a look at how we do control planes these days. Of necessity the data plane is distributed; we have to put interfaces close to the sources and destinations. But our current generation of switches have an attached controller, whether integrated or as a separate hardware device in the same chassis. So the control plane is distributed to the exact same locations as the data plane nodes. That means that the control plane functions (routing, CoS, security, loop avoidance, failure recovery, etc.) require complex cross-network interactions. In the worst case a network with n nodes, in which every node must interact with every other node, requires $n^2 - n$ unidirectional interactions.

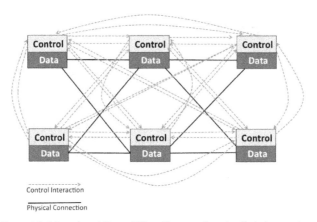

Control Interaction

Physical Connection

Figure 1.5: A Distributed Control Plane Requires Complex Node Interactions

Take OSPF, for example. The algorithm for calculating a shortest-path tree from each node to every other node in the network is simple and fast. The complexity of OSPF is all in the interactions required to establish reliable adjacencies, build the link-state database (LSB), synchronize the LSB with neighbors, and ensure that the entries in the database are current and correct. The "n-squared" complexity of OSPF relationships can be contained by creating areas, but only by sacrificing some precision of route information. News about link state changes takes an appreciable amount of time to be propagated throughout the network, during which black-holes and microloops can occur.

Suppose that every node in the network reports its link state information directly to a centralized controller instead of to every other node in the network. The controller performs a modified SPF calculation and updates the FIBs of each node directly. There is no need to perform complex inter-controller synchronization because there is only the one controller. Transient microloops and black holes are reduced because there is a single control plane view of the network. There is less need for bypass schemes like Fast Reroute (FRR) or Loop-Free Alternates (LFA) to keep traffic flowing while the control plane re-converges after a link or node failure. And a network with n nodes has only n control plane interactions, so as the network grows the number of interactions grows linearly instead of exponentially.

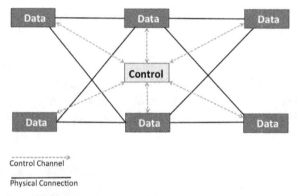

Figure 1.6: A Centralized Control Plane Eliminates Cross-Network Interactions.

This scenario is far from perfect. The effectiveness of centralization declines as the geographic diameter of the network increases; complexity returns as redundant control nodes are distributed; and the expense of direct interaction between a switch and a controller increases with the distance between the two devices.

Nevertheless, the incentives for evaluating SDN solutions and beginning to plan for it are strong:

- **CAPEX Reduction**: Much of the expense of high-performance switches derives from the control plane. Not the controller itself, which is really nothing more than a specialized server, but from the network operating software residing in the controller. This software represents tens of thousands of engineering development hours – one vendor calls their operating system the repository of their collective experience – the cost of which must be recouped. A centralized controller means paying for a network operating system once, instead of every time you purchase a new network node.

- **OPEX Reduction**: Operations are always the largest portion of an IT budget. Humans are expensive. But there is money to be saved if those humans only have to configure services and network parameters at a single control plane interface, rather than having to "touch" each affected device in the network – especially if there are multiple CLI types and operating systems, requiring extensive engineer training.

- **Increased Reliability**: Direct human interaction with the network is a major cause of network outages, and the odds of configuration mistakes narrow directly with the number of devices that must be routinely reconfigured and the number of CLIs that must be used. An SDN controller automates some of this interaction, and ensures consistent configurations. It's important to note that operational policies and procedures serve primarily to set guidelines around human interaction with the network, but are expensive to establish and maintain. SDN can reduce the weight of policies and procedures, having an impact on both reliability and operational expense.

- **Workflow Integration**: Network reconfiguration is an obstacle to virtualization workflows and server / storage / application mobility, especially in the data center. SDN is a beginning toward integrating the network into virtualization management.

- **Agility**: SDN decreases the time required to bring new services online and perform changes in service profiles. There are particular benefits for making cloud services more agile.

- **Accountability and Governance**: SDN allows for centralized policy enforcement at Layers 2 and 3. Controllers can also integrate, through Representational State Transfer (REST) APIs, with Layer 4-7 application policy controllers for both dynamic policy control and more agile adaptation to changing application demands. This integration also has implications for bringing us closer to application-driven networks, discussed later in this chapter.

- **High Availability**: A centralized view of the network, near-real-time network statistics, and the ability to integrate with network analytics can make an SDN controller an important part of an HA design.

A Practical Example: Next-Generation Data Centers

SDN got its start in academic networks at Stanford and a few other universities as a means for researchers to develop network technologies suited to their needs. As chapters 5 and 6 explain, there are diverse use cases for SDN. But presently, the overwhelming adoption of SDN is happening in the data center. It's not hard to see why, considering that until a few years ago most data center networks were still struggling along on technologies that are 15 or more years old.

The greatest bane to data center engineers was – and to a large extent still is – Spanning Tree Protocol (STP, 802.1D). Created to prevent loops in densely connected Layer 2 topologies, STP wastes resources by blocking 50 percent or more of the links in a redundantly-connected network, has terrible failover times, and is prone to misconfiguration.

Over the years there have been many of enhancements to STP to reduce its adverse effects in networks:

- Rapid Spanning Tree Protocol (RSTP, 802.1w), which in some cases reduces the failover times from 30 – 50 seconds to around 6 seconds – still unacceptable in a setting where milliseconds and even microseconds count.

- Multiple Spanning Tree Protocol (MSTP, 802.1s) improves resource utilization by allowing different VLAN groups to elect different roots and built separate spanning trees.

- Link Aggregation Control Protocol (LACP, 802.1ax) bundles multiple parallel links so that STP treats them as a single link.

- Shortest Path Bridging (SPB, 802.1aq) and Transparent Interconnection of Lots of Links (TRILL)[3] utilize shortest path first algorithms normally seen used at Layer 3 to prevent loops and shorten failover times.

These are all just patches on a problematic protocol or, in the case of SPB and TRILL, replacements of STP altogether for a different loop prevention scheme. Consider this: If there were no trees in the topology, there would be no need for Spanning Tree. That is the goal of the switching fabrics introduced by quite a few vendors over recent years.

While the fabric implementations themselves vary considerably from vendor to vendor, the concept is the same: Create a flat, virtualized data plane that either gives the appearance of a single switch interconnecting all top-of-rack / end-of-row (TOR/EOR) access switches in the data center, or else make all the TOR/EOR switches themselves appear to be a single switch. A port on any physical or virtual switch appears as a port to the single switching fabric.

---

[3] One of the developers of TRILL is Radia Perlman, who also invented 802.1D Spanning Tree back in 1990. Perlman was also instrumental in the development of IS-IS, so it is unsurprising that TRILL uses IS-IS.

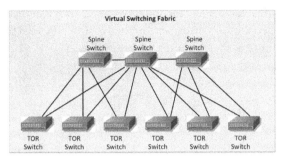

Figure 1.7: Switching Fabrics Create a Flat, Virtualized Data Plane.

There are many compelling reasons, outside the scope of this brief discussion, for moving to a virtual switching fabric in the data center. For our purposes the important point is the evolution of the L2 data plane from a tree of interconnected switches to a single virtualized switch. The switch still consists of multiple physical components, but it behaves like and is managed like a single switch. In other words, the data plane becomes an *abstraction*: We operate the data plane as a whole rather than as a set of loosely connected devices.

Virtualization and Abstraction

You don't have to live in a data center to understand virtualization. If you are a network technologist you deal with virtualization all the time: Virtual Circuits, Virtual LAN, Virtual Private Networks, Virtual Router Redundancy Protocol, Virtual Routing and Forwarding, Virtual Private LAN Service, and on and on. In every case a virtual network entity is something that appears to be real but is not; it is created and represented by physical entities running in the background.

VRRP, for example, provides the appearance of a single router to hosts. The router doesn't really exist; it is represented by two or more real routers that keep an eye on each other to ensure that upstream paths are always available to the hosts. Said differently, the real routers in a VRRP topology are abstracted by the virtual router that the hosts see. Host traffic is still handled by real routers, but a failure in the topology should be invisible to hosts. A backup router takes over the job of representing the virtual router, and forwarding continues.

You can see from this example that the benefit of abstraction is that a user has a consistent view of a function or service, even though the infrastructure providing that function or service might change.

Here's where all this leads: If abstraction provides us with a unified data plane, the control plane of necessity also becomes a unified abstraction. And that gets us closer to SDN Definition #2 at the beginning of this chapter: SDN is a conceptual framework in which networks are treated as abstractions.

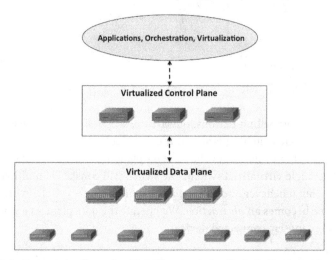

Figure 1.8: An Abstracted or Generalized Data Plane Leads to a Similarly Abstracted Control Plane.

It also removes us a bit from Definition #1. While we think of SDN as a centralized controller – and usually is implemented as one – there is nothing that requires SDN to be a discrete device or server, or even to be centralized. Instead, SDN is a set of software entities that interface with the network.

But we can go even further with this generalization.

On to Network Programmability

Operators interface with the control plane of discrete routers or switches through the Management plane – using a CLI, GUI, SNMP, an XML-based API, or a number of other means – to change configurations, gather statistics, and monitor the device. Said more simply, the Management plane is how the operator and the control plane communicate with each other.

We've already seen how, by treating the underlying data plane as an abstraction, an SDN control plane eliminates the need for an operator to interact with each individual network device. And a "southbound" protocol like OpenFlow eliminates the need for either an operator or the control plane itself to know any vendor-specific language to interact with the data plane.

Similarly, an abstracted control plane provides generalized "northbound" APIs to the Management plane. The operator can program the entire network through a single interface and gather information from the network through a single interface. To understand the importance of this, we turn again to the evolution of data centers.

Virtualization in modern data centers is almost a given. Servers and storage can be built, changed, and moved on the fly, in response to rapidly changing demands. If the data center itself is the business – as is the case with a cloud provider, for example – the ability to *orchestrate* all the moving parts into an agile profit center is essential to business success. Configuration management tools such as Puppet, Salt, Ansible, Chef, and CFEngine have arisen to automate repetitive orchestration tasks among tens to thousands of servers. While these are not true programming languages – they allow you to script routine deployment and management tasks – they do give you the idea of running operations for the entire network through a single CLI rather than individual devices. You specify what you want to happen in one place, and your instructions are executed throughout the network.

Then there are management suites that control a virtualized data center for deploying and managing complete service-oriented infrastructures. One of the best known of these is OpenStack, which is used for deploying cloud services. OpenStack not only allows operators to control their own clouds, cloud providers can make it available to their customers for self-service provisioning and management. It includes software for controlling compute, storage, and networking, plus a dashboard for orchestrating it all. There are other cloud orchestration suites, but because of its strong open support and development community most large cloud providers run OpenStack.

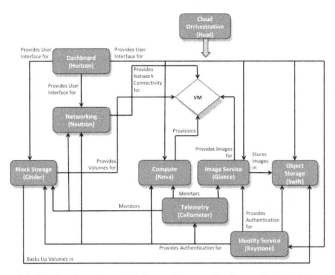

Figure 1.9: OpenStack is a Suite of Software Elements for Controlling Cloud Services.

The popularity of OpenStack undoubtedly is part of the inspiration for an open-source SDN controller developed by the OpenDaylight community. You can see in Figure 1.10 that the OpenDaylight controller can communicate with the data plane via OpenFlow, BGP, LISP, NETCONF, and several other means. Northbound, the user can interface with the controller directly through a GUI or CLI, through OpenStack via Neutron (the OpenStack network program), and other means.

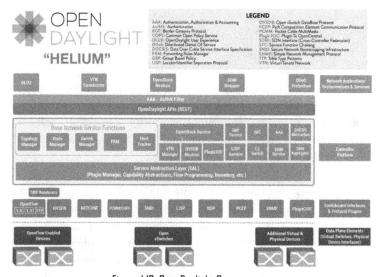

Figure 1.10: OpenDaylight Components.

The example here is not meant to be an endorsement of the OpenDaylight controller – there are many more controllers, both open-source and proprietary. Rather, the example is meant to illustrate how both the data and control planes become abstractions for the purpose of programmability.

Traditional networking involves designing a physical and logical topology, installing and cabling the network nodes, and then configuring each node to conform to your design. It's a static model: If you need to change the network behavior, you have to re-visit the individual nodes and reconfigure them.

SDN allows you to provide "If... Then... Else..." instruction sets to the control plane which then executes the instructions to the data plane. This programmatic approach makes your network much more agile, adaptable, and dynamic. And this is why we've put such emphasis on abstraction. Useful, portable programming depends on abstractions. In the case of SDN, we program to a model of the network – an abstraction – and let the controller deal with the reality.

We've now fully arrived at the second – and more accurate – definition of SDN, so let's repeat it here:

SDN is a conceptual framework in which networks are treated as abstractions and are controlled programmatically, with minimal direct "touch" of individual network components.

Network Function Virtualization

The term "Software Defined Networking" sounds a lot like something that defines elements or functions of the network itself. It's an understandable misconception, but it blurs the definition we've been working on. To keep things clear and simple another term, Network Function Virtualization (NFV), is introduced. NFV has two aspects:

- NFV can be used to define network functions like VPNs, VRFs, tunnels, QoS and security policies, VLANs, and overlays.
- NFV can be used to define, in software, traditionally physical network elements such as routers, L2 switches, firewalls, load balancers, IDS/IPS, and WAN accelerators.

Here's a clean separation of duties:

- SDN programs network *flows*
- NFV programs network *functions*

Naturally, things are not always so clear. There are several foggy areas between these two, such as Traffic Engineering. Do we accomplish TE by programming network flows, or is it defined by programming logical paths through the network? SDN and NFV are new enough that no one can really answer those questions, at least not without a fair amount of civil and uncivil debate. That's because these technologies are still evolving, and the industry itself has not yet arrived at a reliable definition. But development efforts on both SDN and NFV are progressing rapidly, and the industry will provide more concrete definitions in the coming years.

You can easily find people who will disagree with these definitions, and that's fine. We only need the differentiation to help us through the discussions in this book.

Genetic Diversity

Curiously, SDN and NFV have different heritages but are synergizing. SDN got its start in academia, and quickly found practical applications in the data center (Google, Amazon, and a few other massive data center operators were the first non-academic adopters). It's now moving out of the data centers and into WANs, telephony, mobile, and service provider networks.

Large carriers and telephony providers, on the other hand, launched NFV through the European Telecommunications Standards Institute (ETSI). Its genes are rooted in the telephony world, but NFV applications are quickly moving into data centers and cloud provider networks.

SDN and NFV can be used separately, but together they will transform the way we build and operate networks.

Is SDN a Disruptive Technology?

SDN and NFV are catalysts for a sea change in networking. We're moving to a world in which the networks we deal with are abstract, virtual, and defined more by the flows they carry than by the individual links and nodes that make them up. For years we've drawn clouds to represent the network. Well, now the cloud is here.

SDN is not just a disruptive technology. It may well be the most disruptive technology we've seen since the advent of TCP/IP.

Disrupted Operations

SDN does more than just change the way we interact with networks. Any good network management system does that. SDN changes our view of the network from a graph of interconnected nodes to a system of flows between endpoints. We no longer interact with individual devices and links, but instead interact holistically with the network. Add NFV into the mix, and even individual network functions become virtual entities rather than physical devices.

Disrupted Financial Models

Incumbent router and switch vendors have deep engineering investments in their control plane software. Every time you buy a router or switch, you pay for the same operating system, contributing to the vendor's Return on Investment.

SDN changes that model, to one in which you pay for the network operating system once (or perhaps a few times), and build your data plane using "bare metal" devices with either no operating system or a minimally installed operating system.

It's easy to see, given this view of the future of the industry, why incumbent vendors would like to control the SDN conversation, redefine SDN, or change the subject completely.

Disrupted Skill Sets

We've already seen how virtualization in the data center has disrupted job descriptions and skill sets. Where once Application Developers and Operations Engineers were separate jobs (and occasionally at odds with each other), virtualization has enabled their consolidation into DevOps – developers can spin up the compute and storage resources they need without having to coordinate operations specialists.

What's missing out of the current DevOps picture is networking, and SDN is changing that. To the extent that SDN and NFV eventually enables virtualized network elements and zero-touch provisioning, "CLI jockeys" – heavily certified in vendor-specific network operating systems – will be much less in demand. Networking will become more tightly integrated with applications, and network engineers will become network programmers.

On to Application Defined Networks

SDN and NFV could lead to the ultimate disruption: the elimination of human intervention in the network at all. Not to the extent that humans are no longer needed to design, build, and maintain the network, of course, but to the extent that humans are needed to adapt the network to applications, or to adapt applications to the network.

Think about it. Right now, the "human layer" between the network and the applications running on it serves as an arbiter: We analyze what applications need to run, what network resources are available, and then configure the best compromise we can. Right now, SDN and NFV enable the orchestration of the network based on programmable parameters and collected network information. With SDN firmly in place, we can create applications that interact directly with the orchestration layer.

We already have application aware networking – at least to some degree. But that puts the cart before the horse. Networks exist to support applications, so which is better: Networks that monitor applications and deduce what they need, or applications that tell the network exactly what they need?

Imagine networks that dynamically adjust to real-time application requirements. Application Defined Networks could well be the next disruptive wave following SDN.

Conclusion

In this chapter a base set of fundaments of SDN have been demonstrated. Understanding the importance of the separation of the control and data planes is the key tenant of SDN as a whole, though there are many ways to accomplish this.

After reading this chapter it should be apparent that there is a significant business case to be made for SDN and NFV. Datacenters see an obvious benefit with regards to the ability to better scale and offer far more efficient use of resources. Service Providers can utilize NFV as a value added service, generating significant revenue for the organization.

The rest of this book will focus on the concept of open SDN, and specifically detail the history and function of the OpenFlow protocol.

2

SDN Overview

This chapter takes a look at the origins of SDN, lays out a reference architecture and talks about some of the early adopters. It is very important to note that we are discussing the history of SDN and how it relates to OpenFlow, a protocol within the SDN architecture. An examination of applicable research indicates that the term "Software Defined Networking" was first coined by Katie Green in March 2009; however, the concept was discussed long before the term SDN became mainstream

> For her article check out this link:
> http://www2.technologyreview.com/article/412194/tr10-software-defined-networking/

The Origins of SDN

SDN Drivers

The Internet as we know it today could not have been predicted; the Internet is a large collection of different companies, network devices, and protocols all trying their best to work together. At each stage in networking history, different protocols have been written and chosen to solve the problem of the day. Currently, we can identify several general network trends that are key drivers to SDN:

1. Ethernet is not quite everywhere but is almost everywhere and someday soon will be.
2. x86 processors are widely deployed and understood.

3. Most network links could be better utilized with more network flow intelligence.
4. Most Layer 2 and Layer 3 network devices are closed systems.

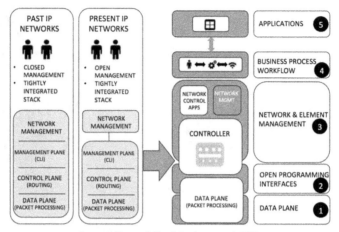

Figure 1. Network Stack Evolution with SDN

Looking at Figure 1, we can see where network devices have moved from closed management and integration stacks to a more open management stack. Protocols based on XML such as NETCONF have been key drivers in opening up the management, provisioning, and automation of these devices. However, the integration stack of the devices still remains closed. In the SDN architecture we are trying to open this stack up to provide more programmability and align with business, process, and policy flow for the organization. Essentially, we are trying to create an open system for management services and the control plane. Before we dive into this architecture let's look at a little bit of history of where SDN and specifically a protocol within SDN, OpenFlow came from today.

OpenFlow History

The Origins of OpenFlow can be traced back to 2006, when Martin Casado, a PhD student at Stanford developed something called Ethane. He was working with Professor Nick Mckeown as part of the Clean Slate program.

Clean Slate Program

The Clean Slate program was designed to answer this question: "What would the Internet look like in 15 years if we started with a clean slate?" The research also closely complemented two projects of the National Science Foundation.

The first, called GENI, for Global Environment for Network Innovations (http://www.geni.net/), aims to build a nationwide programmable platform for research in network architectures. The second, called FIND, for Future Internet Network Design (http://find.isi.edu/), aims to develop new Internet architectures.

The Clean Slate program coordinators looked at several key areas for research:

- Network Architecture
- Heterogeneous Applications
- Heterogeneous Physical-Layer technologies
- Network Security
- Economics and Policy

This program has now ceased to exist but has produced some key follow-up programs:

1. OpenFlow and SDN
2. POMI 2020 for Mobile Programmability
3. Social Media for Mobile: MobiSocial
4. Stanford Experimental Lab

Casado was trying to figure out a way to centrally manage global policy with a network that was dynamic and non-symmetrical. In other words, how do you keep track of the state of the network (something that OSPF did well) to drive programmability and enforcement of network policies? So his group at Stanford (Michael J. Freedman, Justin Pettit, Jianying Luo, and Nick McKeown) along with Scott Shenker at Berkeley set forth to create a controller that manages network state and drives forwarding changes based on the policies set forth; thus OpenFlow and centralized controllers were born.

For more information on Ethane, see this paper: Ethane: Taking Control of the Enterprise: http://www.cs.utexas.edu/users/yzhang/teaching/cs386m-f8/Readings/fp298-casado.pdf .

SDN Reference Architecture

Now that we see where this idea came from, it is time to take a step back and actually talk about the idea itself and a few definitions. The idea of SDN is to create a programmable network, and this programmable network has a few key frameworks:

1. Contains a programmable Control plane
2. It contains formal protocols and specifications
3. It allows for Data plane abstraction
4. It allows for virtualization of the underlying network

Figure 2 displays the SDN reference architecture, which consists of the "simple" packet forwarding architecture, a network operating system and a well-defined API. The idea relates back to Figure 1 in the network stack evolution as we begin to open the network stack inside the router/switch and firewall and bring up the intelligence into a network operating system. How much intelligence should be in the network OS is still under debate, but all agree that it should contain state information that is passed down to the packet forwarding devices. When this architecture is examined there are three places where formal protocols and specifications could occur.

1. The interface from the network operating system to the packet forwarding hardware
2. The network operating system itself
3. The API above the network operating system

As of 2015 the network operating system runs on a device called a controller, which could be proprietary or open source. The packet forwarding hardware can be devices from Cisco, Juniper, Brocade, Arista or other network vendors, or it could also be an open source device (whitebox) or a virtual device like a vSwitch. The APIs are still under development, and will be discussed later in this book

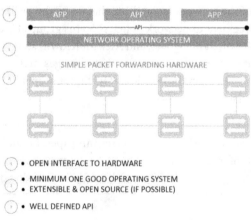

Figure 2. SDN Reference Architecture

Figure 3 shows a deeper breakdown of the SDN architecture. Often people will refer to SDN with directions such as southbound, northbound etc. These are software directions from the reference point of the network operating system:

- Northbound interface: In computer networking and computer architecture, a northbound interface of a component is an interface that conceptualizes the lower-level details (e.g., data or functions) used by, or in, the component. In the SDN architecture this will be APIs toward an orchestration system.

- Southbound interface: Allows a particular network component to communicate with a lower-level component. In the SDN architecture this can be a protocol such as OpenFlow.

- East-West interface: Communicate between groups or federations of controllers to synchronize state for high availability. This protocol has yet to be standardized.

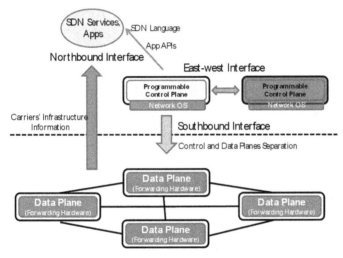

Figure 3. SDN Software Architecture

SDN Definitions

So, are we clearer to defining what SDN is? Searching the Internet may bring up some of the definitions below.

Definition 1:
Software-defined networking (SDN) is an approach to networking in which control is decoupled from hardware and given to a software application called a controller.

Definition 2:
SDN is a technology to networking that allows centralized, programmable control planes so that network operators can control and manage directly their own virtualized networks.

Doug Marschke, Jeff Doyle and Pete Moyer

Definition 3:
SDN is implementing network functionality in software that does not run on network devices.

All of these definitions have one thing in common: they all have their basis around the separation of the control plane. SDN is more than just a discussion of centralized control planes, and more a realization that what we expect of a Layer 3 forwarding device has changed. Long ago are the days that wire rate forwarding is not the norm. So what currently differentiates one vendor from another, except for their OS and underlying software features?

SDN can be defined as a network architecture that opens up a network to programmability and traffic control from one or more central control points. The idea is to change the way we design networks and provide an open programmable interface to change the way traffic flows through the forwarding device. (Recall Figure 2.)

Standards Bodies Update

A variety of standards bodies and organizations are attempting to standardize the protocols needed for the SDN architecture. These include but are not limited to:

1. ONF (Open Networking Foundation)
2. OpenDaylight
3. IETF
4. NFV/ETSI

Open Networking Foundation

The ONF formed in 2011 and it can be considered one of the founding organizations for SDN. The ONF consists of members that contribute to the working groups of the ONF. The ONF's original responsibility was taking over the OpenFlow switch standardization. This is a standard that informs switches where to send packets and is the focus of chapters 3 and 4.

Other definitions include OpenFlow Config and OpenFlow Test. OpenFlow config is a complementary protocol that defines the mechanism for OpenFlow controllers to configure open flow switches. OpenFlow Test is a Python based OpenFlow switch test framework and collection of test cases. It is based on unittest, which is included in the standard Python distribution.

As the ONF evolves into an organization, more working groups are being formed. Here are the current working groups:

- Architecture and Framework: The Architecture and Framework working group was created to help standardize SDN by defining the broad set of problems that the SDN architecture needs to address

- Configuration and Management: The Configuration and Management working group (CMWG) was created to address core Operations, Administration, and Management (OA&M) issues with the OpenFlow Standard.

- Extensibility: The Extensibility working group is developing extensions to the OpenFlow switch protocol that best take advantage of the latest innovations to promote OpenFlow Standard adoption.

- Forwarding Abstraction: OpenFlow Standard versions up through 1.3 describe a framework in which controllers request switch forwarding behavior step-by-step (flowmod-by-flowmod) at runtime. The Hardware Abstraction Layer (HAL) must be capable of mapping individual flowmods on the fly to the underlying hardware platform. The Forwarding Abstractions working group (FAWG) is evolving the HAL specifications to simplify the implementation process of the OpenFlow Standard and improve the flexibility of target HALs.

- Market Education: The Market Education Committee (MEC) is the outbound facing arm of the ONF. Our primary goals are to educate the SDN community on the value proposition of software-defined networks based on the OpenFlow Standard and promoting adoption of ONF Standards. In addition, the MEC is responsible for channeling market feedback to guide the technical working groups, and focusing on use case definition and high-level market requirement development

- Migration: The Migration working group will produce methods to migrate network service from a traditional network, like a data center or a wide area network, to a Software-Defined Network (SDN) based on the OpenFlow Standard. This group will bring together practitioners who have carried out or have interest in carrying out software-defined network migrations.

- Northbound Interface: The Northbound Interfaces (NBI) working group was created to help develop concrete requirements, architecture, and working code for northbound interface

- Optical Transport: The Optical Transport working group will address SDN and OpenFlow Standard-based control capabilities for optical transport networks. The work will include identifying use cases, defining a target reference architecture for controlling optical transport networks incorporating the OpenFlow Standard, and identifying and creating OpenFlow protocol extensions.

- Testing and Interoperability: The Testing and Interoperability working group seeks to accelerate the development and adoption of the OpenFlow Standard. The group will work toward this goal by ensuring standardized development through testing and certification, fostering interoperability among vendor implementations, and providing an industry-recognized certification for ONF compliance.

- Wireless and Mobile: The Wireless and Mobile working group discusses progression of methods by which OpenFlow can be used to control wireless Radio Area Networks (RAN) and core networks.

OpenDaylight

Formed in 2013, OpenDaylight is a collaborative open source project hosted by the Linux foundation. The goal of OpenDaylight is not necessarily to create a standard but produce a working code. This working code can be used to create a working SDN (and NFV) environment.

Figure 4 shows the framework of OpenDaylight projects. At its core the goal is to have an SDN controller at its core that can be run on any piece of hardware or software that supports Java. The controller will contain multiple software packages that perform various functions as well as northbound (restful APIs) and southbound APIs. The Southbound is dynamically linked to the Service Abstraction Layer (SAL).

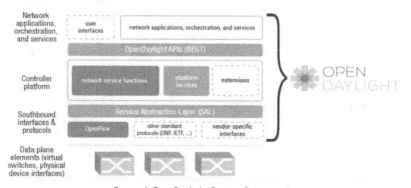

Figure 4. OpenDaylight Project Framework

Projects will continue to form at Open Daylight and the project is ever-evolving. Just by way of example, some of the projects at Open Daylight include:

- OpenDaylight Controller
- OpenDaylight Network Virtualization Platform
- OpenDaylight Virtual Tenant Network (VTN)
- Open DOVE
- OpenFlow Plugin
- Affinity Metadata Service

The Hydrogen release of OpenDaylight represents OpenDaylight's first official working SDN controller, and has since been replaced by the Helium release in 2014.

Internet Engineering Task Force (IETF)

The IETF is often considered the grandfather of Internet standards bodies, particularly as it relates to all things TCP/IP. The IETF is where you will see the standards from our favorite routing protocols such as OSPF and BGP.

The IETF originally took a back seat in the SDN standards process, as SDN was not necessarily changing protocols for use in the TCP/IP stack. However, as the SDN architecture becomes more widely accepted, several workgroups have started that affect pieces of the SDN architecture, such as the SDN Research group, Interface to Routing Systems, and Application Layer Traffic Optimization.

For example, the goal of the Interface to Routing Systems (I2RS) from the charter is:

> "I2RS facilitates real-time or event driven interaction with the routing system through a collection of protocol-based control or management interfaces. These allow information, policies, and operational parameters to be injected into and retrieved (as read or by notification) from the routing system while retaining data consistency and coherency across the routers and routing infrastructure, and among multiple interactions with the routing system. The I2RS interfaces will co-exist with existing configuration and management systems and interfaces."

At the time of this writing, the group has not fully fleshed out the protocols they are going to support, but hopefully they will by the time we write volume two!

Network Function Virtualization and ETSI

Related to SDN is Network Function Virtualization (NFV), which was briefly discussed in Chapter 1. Recall that NFV's basic idea is to break out commercialized hardware for IT and network function onto a single machine or series of machines.

While NFV builds the virtualized network functions it does not define the network to support them. This is where the SDN architecture comes in.

The European Telecommunications Standards Institute (ETSI) is an independent, non-profit standards body. It is well known for creating standards such as the Global System for Mobile Communications (GSM) phone network and low power device (LPD) radio.

In late 2012 several providers came together to form a group within ETSI to define the requirements and architecture for the virtualization of network functions.

Early Commercial Developers and Adopters

So was any of this theory put to use? The short answer is yes! There were some early adopters that paved the way for SDN deployments and two of these are highlighted in the following pages, Google and NTT. Although many other deployments exist, we decided to discuss these now due to the large amount of public information on these deployments. Other deployments will be described in later chapters.

Google

One of the most well known deployments was the deployment at Google. They were such an early adopter that they had to build their own network gear as there was no commercial product available at the time.

Before describing the Google case, let us give a little background about their network. Google essentially operates two backbones, the Internet facing backbone and the data center backbone. The Internet facing backbone is the user traffic we all know, and the data center backbone is internal traffic. The early OpenFlow deployment was on the data center backbone.

Google was noticing a trend that the cost/bit was not decreasing as the network grew but actually increasing! This was due to manual management and configuration of the larger (and more expensive) network boxes and the automation complexity of having to deal with vendor non-standard APIs.

Google's solution was to manage the WAN as a fabric and not as a collection of individual boxes. The problem was that current protocols did not support this and there was little support for low latency routing and fast failovers.

Consider the network example in Figure 5. Imagine you have the following flows: MPLS label switched paths (LSP) in red, green, and purple. The values in the diagram represent the available reservation bandwidth available. All of the flows require 20 Mbps as a reservation They all share the common link between R5 and R6, and the "best" link fails between R5 and R6. This will cause R1, R2, and R4 to find a new best path.

- **Flows:** R1->R6: 20; R2->R6: 20; R4->R6: 20

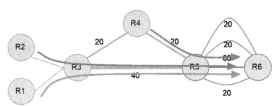

Figure 5. Flows

Imagine R1 finds the best path first, and then R2 and R4 begin the race to find the next best path. R2 wins this round and R4 tries again. Finally R4 gets the third best path.

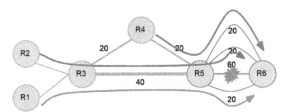

- **R5-R6 link fails**
  - R1, R2, R4 *autonomously* try for next best path
  - R1 wins, R2, R4 retry for next best path
  - R2 wins this round, R4 retries again
  - R4 finally gets third best path

Figure 6. Path Failure

Eventually all three LSPs find a path, but two results of the outcome were that the LSP that got the first path was non-deterministic and the time it took R4 to find its path was insignificant. One could argue there could be ways to solve this issue with priorities, yet there is still a timing, a setup, and a tear down element that can't be ignored. The Google solution was to create a centralized controller to solve this problem. (Figure 7)

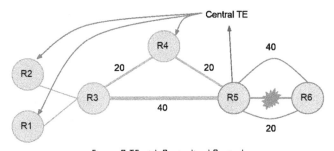

Figure 7. TE with Centralized Control

In the example when the link between R5 and R6 fails, R5 informs the Central TE. All of the routers are programmed in one shot, which leads to a faster realization of the optimum paths.

Google then moved on to the idea of building the central controller. They needed a language to speak to the controller and for that purpose they chose OpenFlow. The controller uses modern server hardware, and the forwarding elements were devices made from standard merchant silicon. (Figure 8). These non-blocking 10G devices used open source routing stacks (BGP and ISIS) such as quagga and had OpenFlow support.

Figure 8. Google router/switch

Of course the migration to this new network had to take place in phases. The OpenFlow switches at first looked like regular routers as ISIS neighbors. Next, the controller was BGP peer to program the switch state. Then the network slowly turned down peers until all network elements were converged on to the new OpenFlow network.

After the new network was fully deployed, Google saw increased link utilization, faster deployment and in service and hitless software upgrades and easy feature additions.

We all don't have the resources that Google had to build their own switches and routers, but they did lay the groundwork to show that SDN with OpenFlow was possible.

NTT

Another early adopter of SDN was NTT, which looked at a different use case for deployment, which they called "automation for GW interconnection." Essentially they wanted to find a way to improve their VPN offering to their customers. They used MPLS/BGP VPNs and connected to a variety of data centers for some services. Whenever they rolled out a new customer they would need to issue complicated commands on the VPN routers in order to establish connectivity. (Figure 9)

NTT decided to roll out an SDN architecture (Figure 9). NTT used an OpenFlow switch on the edge based on the Open vSwitch (OVS) and home-grown OpenFlow controller running over Ryu. They basically wanted the SDN controller to communicate with the data center edge devices and the MPLS cloud edge devices (Figure 10). A portal (SDN application) spawns a new VPN, which communicates to the controller over and API. The controller then provisions the edge devices to enable this connectivity. This is a combination of OpenFlow rules sent to the controller as well as configuration commands for the devices themselves. Additionally the SDN controller is a BGP peer for the BGP/MPLS network.

Figure 9. NTT SDN View

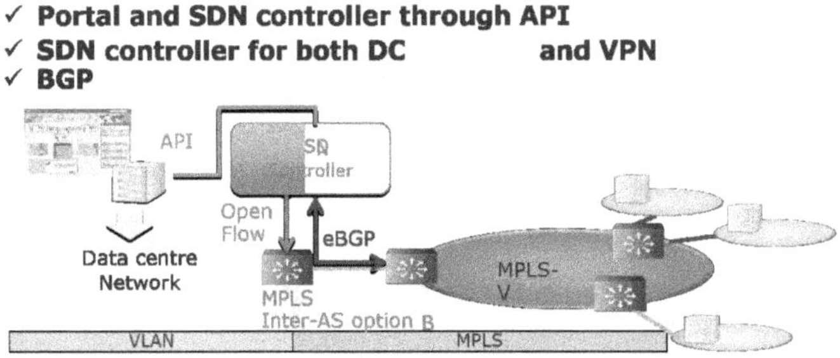

✓ **Portal and SDN controller through API**
✓ **SDN controller for both DC   and VPN**
✓ **BGP**

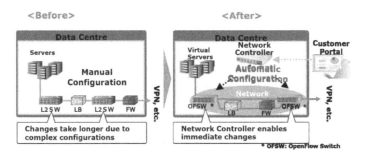

Figure 10. NTT Interconnection

As an example, let's look at the BGP and OpenFlow interaction in the MPLS networks.

The customer edge devices still connect to the PE devices as before; however, the BGP sessions are not handled by the PE but by a BGP route controller in the network. The OpenFlow controller had already pre-programmed flows that would allow all BGP control traffic to the BGP controller.

The ONF's migration document describes this behavior, which I will repeat here: (Figure 11)

The role of the BGP route controller is similar to a route reflector for eBGP neighbors. Incoming BGP sessions are recognized by the OpenFlow agent and forwarded to BGP route controllers in the network. The BGP route controller manages BGP sessions with the peering routers; however, no end customer or Internet traffic flows to/from the peers into the network until the flow table is programmed by the OpenFlow Agent at the edge device.

The OpenFlow Agent redirects the BGP session to the BGP route controller without changing anything in the packet, using the default OpenFlow match entry. From a physical connectivity point of view, the BGP route controller may or may not be directly connected to the OpenFlow Agent and it may service multiple OpenFlow Agents. For each BGP session, the BGP route controller must be configured with a VLAN and the corresponding IP address (e.g.,. A', B' and C'), which is configured on the device.

To populate the forwarding plane, the OpenFlow Controller needs a copy of the BGP routing information. It gets the routing information from the BGP route controller and builds a flow table, which is then pushed to the OpenFlow Agent. Once flows are programmed successfully, traffic can be forwarded through the edge device without running BGP on it. Any changes (i.e., updates) processed by the route controller are reflected in the OpenFlow controller, which, in turn, updates the flow table through the OpenFlow Agent accordingly.

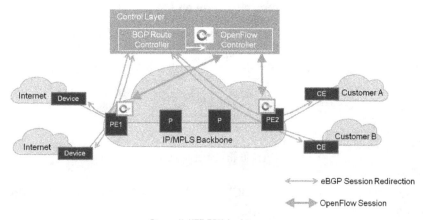

Figure 11. NTT SDN Architecture

Figure 12 shows the architecture design goals for NTT. A few points of interest: NTT makes use of "SDN Applications."

The SDN common framework includes a controller as well other APIs and drivers. The forwarding elements are OpenFlow capable and thus could be vendor-neutral.

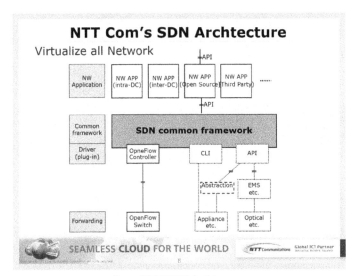

Figure 12. NTT SDN Architecture

OpenFlow and Its Alternatives

Although this volume concentrates on OpenFlow, we know that it is not the only southbound protocol out there. In fact, later volumes of this series will look at some of the other options.

For example, Juniper's SDN solution called Contrail currently uses a combination of Extensible Messaging and Presence Protocol (XMPP) and BGP and eliminates OpenFlow. We will not debate the merits of this solution in this volume but we will look at these solutions in more detail in later volumes.

Conclusion

In this chapter the history of OpenFlow was explored, and the hard work and dedication by the Open Networking Foundation and those involved with the OpenDaylight project was detailed.

Furthermore, a number of case studies for SDN deployments in the wild were discussed. Traffic Engineering enhancements were a focus in many of the larger deployments. Based on these examples it is clear that SDN is certainly conceptually viable.

3

OpenFlow Overview

Introduction

There are a number of ways to view OpenFlow: as a protocol, as an instruction set, or as an architecture. It's all of those things. Formally, OpenFlow defines an interface between an SDN controller and a switch. Within the larger context of SDN, it's the "southbound" interface of the controller.[4]

OpenFlow is not alone in that role. There are alternative messaging protocols and alternative means of communication between the controller and the switch. So while this chapter is devoted to the gears and levers of OpenFlow, you should be aware that OpenFlow is not the only game in town.

OpenFlow Standards

OpenFlow standards are specified by the Open Networking Foundation (ONF),[5] a non-profit organization founded in early 2011 by Microsoft, Google, Verizon, Yahoo!, Deutsche Telekom, and Facebook. Those six companies, plus Goldman Sachs and NTT Communications, supply the board members managing ONF. And those companies –telecoms, Internet carriers, an investment banking firm, content

---

[4] Following that convention, the "northbound" interface of the controller connects to users or applications accessing the SDN control plane. In fact one of the working groups of the Open Networking Foundation is the Northbound Interface Working Group. You can also think of "East-West" interfaces, which – predictably – interconnect controllers.

[5] www.opennetworking.org

providers, social media providers, and operators of some of the world's most massive data centers – give you a pretty good perspective on the industry interest in SDN. As this book is being written ONF has around 150 member organizations, collaborating to promote SDN and to develop open SDN standards.

OpenFlow is specified in a number of documents:

- *OpenFlow Switch Specification* describes the OpenFlow Protocol – the protocol the controller and switch use to communicate with each other – and the requirements of an OpenFlow Logical Switch.

- *OpenFlow Management and Configuration Protocol* specifies the configuration and management protocol – OF-CONFIG – used to communicate between a remote OpenFlow configuration point and an operational context supporting an OpenFlow Switch. The relationship between a controller, a configuration point, and a switch is illustrated in Figure 3.1. An OpenFlow operation context is an OpenFlow-capable switch supporting one or more OpenFlow Logical Switches.

- *OpenFlow Notifications Framework* specifies how OpenFlow capable switches (Notification Publishers) notify OpenFlow Configuration Points, OpenFlow Controllers, or possibly other northbound management entities of switch events.

- *OpenFlow Controller-Switch NDM Specification* describes how an OpenFlow Control Point can use OF-CONFIG to negotiate a Negotiable Datapath Model (NDM) with an OpenFlow Capable Switch.

- *OpenFlow Table Type Patterns* specifies abstract switch models, called Table Type Patterns (TTPs), which describe specific switch forwarding behaviors and flow processing capabilities of an OpenFlow Logical Switch that a controller can program. The goals of TTPs are to assist product interoperability and simplify the development process.

- *OpenFlow Conformance Test Specification* describes test procedures to verify conformance to OpenFlow switch specifications.

Most of these documents exist in multiple versions, although as of this writing none of them have moved beyond a subset of version 1.x. This chapter describes the OpenFlow switch protocol, with just a few elements of OF-CONFIG thrown in. Although there is a version 1.4.0 of the OpenFlow Switch Specification, the version currently in most common use is 1.3.x. In fact there are minor versions of 1.3, comprising fixes and clarifications, which have been released more recently than 1.4.0.

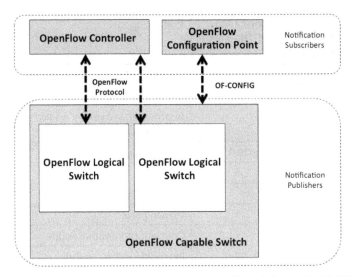

Figure 3.1: The OpenFlow Protocol is used between the controller and the switch, while OF-CONFIG is used between a configuration point and the operation context supporting the switch.

Table 3.1 lists the most important features released in each version and sub-version of the OpenFlow Switch Specification, beginning with version 1.0.0. There are releases predating this – versions 0.2.0 through 0.9 – but we treat these as the core OpenFlow specification. The assumption is that any version of OpenFlow you might run will be release 1.0 or higher; if an aspect of OpenFlow is discussed in this chapter without specifying what version it was released in, you can assume that it is supported in all versions.

The list is far from comprehensive – if you need a complete listing of features per release, you can find them in the appendices of each release. We endeavor in this chapter to tell you what version introduces any feature, function, or capability we discuss beyond the core OpenFlow specification, but we also encourage you to refer back to Table 3.1 as needed.

Table 3.1: OpenFlow Switch Specification Versions

Version	Wire Protocol Number	Release Date MM/DD/YYYY	Feature
1.0.0	0x01	12/31/2009	Slicing
			Flow cookies
			User-specifiable datapath description
			Match on IP fields in ARP packets

Version	Wire Protocol Number	Release Date MM/DD/YYYY	Feature
			Match on IP ToS/DSCP bits
			Query port stats for individual ports
			Improved flow duration resolution in stats/ expiry messages
1.1.0	0x02	02/28/2011	Multiple tables (pipelines)
			Groups
			MPLS and VLAN tags
			Virtual ports
			Controller connection failure
1.2	0x03	02/05/2011	Extensible match support
			Extensible "set_field" packet rewriting support
			Extensible context expression in "packet-in"
			Extensible Error messages via experimenter error type
			IPv6 support
			Simplified behavior of flow-mod request
			Removed packet parsing specification
			Controller role change mechanism
1.3.0	0x04	04/13/2012	Refactor capabilities negotiation
			More flexible table miss support
			IPv6 extension header handling
			Per flow meters
			Per connection event filtering
			Auxiliary connections
			MPLS Bottom of Stack (BoS) matching
			Provider Backbone Bridging (PBB) tagging
			Less restrictive tag order
			Tunnel-ID metadata
			Cookies in packet-in
			Duration for stats
			On-demand flow counters
1.3.1	0x04	09/06/2012	Improved version negotiation

Version	Wire Protocol Number	Release Date MM/DD/YYYY	Feature
1.3.2	0x04	04/25/2013	Assorted feature fixes and rule clarifications
1.3.3	0x04	09/27/2013	Assorted feature fixes and rule clarifications
1.3.4	0x04	03/27/2014	Assorted feature fixes and rule clarifications
1.4.0	0x05	10/14/2013	More extensible wire protocol
			More descriptive reasons for packet-in
			Optical port properties
			Flow-removed reason for meter delete
			Flow monitoring
			Role status events
			Eviction
			Vacancy events
			Bundles
			Synchronized tables
			Group and Meter change notifications
			Error code for bad priority
			Error code for Set-async-config
			PBB Use Customer Address (UCC) field
			Error code for duplicate instruction
			Error code for multipart timeout
			Change default TCP port to 6653 (from 6633 and 976, used by previous versions)

Like so many protocols, explaining OF for the first time – at least, outside of formal technical specifications – can be an exercise in convolution. Every component depends on other components, so what should we describe first?

The answer is often to do multiple sweeps across the entire protocol structure, going deeper at each pass. And that's what we'll do in this chapter. We start by looking at a "holistic" view of the OpenFlow components, what each component is, and how they all interrelate. From there we can dig deeper into each component and its constituent *subcomponents*. That, then, allows us to step back and revisit the overall structure and component interrelationships, but with a more sophisticated understanding of each.

OpenFlow Components

Figure 3.2 is a repeat of the diagram of the basic OpenFlow components you saw in Chapter 1 (Figure 1.4). These most fundamental components are:

- OpenFlow Controller
- OpenFlow Logical Switch, which contains:
    - Ports
    - OpenFlow Secure Channel
    - Flow Table, containing a set of flow instructions -- *flow entries* – that tell the switch how to handle a given packet

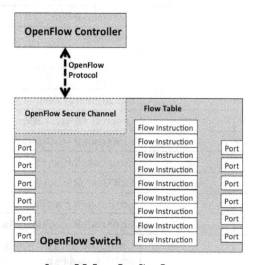

Figure 3.2: Basic OpenFlow Components

We'll introduce a few more basic components in this section:

- Group Table
- Meter Table
- Pipeline

Groups, meter tables, and pipelining expand the diagram of Figure 3.2 in some way, so to keep things simple we'll discuss the fundamental components and then expand Figure 3.2 as each of the last three components are introduced. The remainder of this chapter then digs deeper into how these components work, individually and together.

Controller

Although the controller is vital to any SDN architecture, it is somewhat peripheral to the OpenFlow architecture. Almost everything we are interested in, in the context of OpenFlow, happens "south" of the controller.

The OpenFlow component in the controller is responsible for communicating instructions to the switch across the Secure Channel, but the OpenFlow protocol has no say in how the controller determines what instructions to send. All of that happens at a higher layer within or above the controller. The instructions might be determined by an automated orchestration component, by direct operator intervention, or by traditional path determination protocols such as OSPF or BGP.

In fact OpenFlow might not be the only southbound communications protocol used by the controller. It might communicate with other switches, or even the same switch, using some other open or proprietary protocol.

Switch

The switch is where almost everything of interest to us in this chapter happens. Packet processing happens through a set of tables: flow tables, a group table, and a meter table. The tables are populated with instructions from the controller through the OpenFlow channel. Packets enter and exit processing through ports, just as they would in a normal switch.

The switch diagrammed in Figure 3.2 is an OpenFlow logical switch. Looking at Figure 3.1, you can see that a single OpenFlow capable switch can support multiple OpenFlow logical switches. Moving forward in this chapter, when we refer to a switch, we mean an OpenFlow logical switch.

A switch can also be either an OpenFlow-only switch or a hybrid switch:

- An *OpenFlow-only* switch, as the name suggests, can only process and forward packets using the components and processes described in this chapter.

- A *hybrid* switch supports both OpenFlow and traditional Ethernet switching, which can include not only L2 switching and VLANs, but also L3 IPv4 and IPv6 routing.

Whether a switch is OpenFlow-only or hybrid makes a difference in some port functions, as described in the next subsection.

Ports

Ports on an OpenFlow switch serve the same input/output purpose that they do on any switch. Packets are received on an *ingress* or *input* port, are processed, and switched to an *egress* or *output* port. (Whether you prefer the ingress/egress or input/output nomenclature is entirely your choice. They mean the same thing.) Ingress and egress are defined from the perspective of a packet flow: The ingress port for one flow might be the output port for another flow. Again, this is no different from any other switch.

A port can be added, changed, or removed in the switch configuration using, for example, OF-CONFIG or directly from the controller. A port state can also change, such as when a link goes down or comes up. Port changes do not change a flow entry pointing to that port. So for example, if a port goes down or is removed and a flow entry directs packets to that port, the packets are dropped. For this reason port changes must be communicated to the controller so that the controller can clean up any flow entries related to the port.

OpenFlow defines three types of *standard ports*, and an OpenFlow switch must support all three:

- Physical ports
- Logical ports
- Reserved ports

While the concept of physical, logical, and reserved ports exist in earlier switch specifications, they are first spelled out clearly in 1.2.

Physical Ports

Physical ports correspond directly to the hardware interfaces on a switch. When a physical switch supports multiple OpenFlow logical switches, the hardware interfaces might be shared among several or all of the logical switches. In this case, the OpenFlow physical port on a logical switch is a virtual slice of the corresponding physical interface. Conceptually, this virtual slice is like a VLAN, sub-interface, or logical interface unit: A single physical interface can support multiple virtual physical ports.

Logical Ports

Logical ports do not correspond directly to hardware interfaces. They include the kinds of logical interfaces you encounter on any kind of L2 or L3 switch, such as tunnel interfaces, loopback interfaces, null interfaces, MPLS LSPs, and link aggregation groups. The packet handling of a logical port, such as encapsulation / de-capsulation and whether it maps to a hardware interface, is implementation-specific and independent of OpenFlow. From the perspective of the OpenFlow processes, a logical port is usually treated the same as a physical port.[6]

Reserved Ports

Reserved ports are ports used for internal packet processing, for special functions such as flooding, or in a hybrid switch, for handoff from an OpenFlow logical switch to the "normal" switching process. Reserved ports can be either *required* or *optional*.

The Required ports are:

- **ALL** includes all ports that can be used as output ports. From the perspective of directional packet flow, ALL includes all ports except the input port and any ports configured not to forward packets. When a packet is flooded, it is sent to the ALL port.

- **CONTROLLER** is the port in the Secure Channel that connects the switch to the controller, and can be either an ingress or output port. When the CONTROLLER is an ingress port, it receives OpenFlow messages from the controller; when it is an output port, it encapsulates packets in a *packet-in* message and sends it to the controller.

- **TABLE** is the ingress port to a pipeline, as described later in this section.

- **IN_PORT** seems counter-intuitive, at first. It is a packet's ingress port, but it can be used only as an output port. It is used when a packet must be sent back out the port on which it was received.

- **ANY** is used neither as an ingress nor an output port, but can represent any or all ports. It is a special port used when an OpenFlow request requires a port specification but no other port can be specified. In this sense it can be thought of as just a functional placeholder.

The Optional ports are:

- **LOCAL** is the ingress and egress of the switch's local networking and management stacks.

---

[6] There are a few instances of packet handling in which packets from a logical port may require some identification in addition to the identification of packets from a physical port.

- **NORMAL** is supported only in hybrid switches. This is the output port from the OpenFlow process to the normal switch process.

- **FLOOD**, like NORMAL, is only supported in hybrid switches, and is output only. Packets to be flooded by the normal switching process—either to all egress hardware interfaces or to a set of egress VLAN ports—are sent to FLOOD.

Secure Channel

The OpenFlow channel is the communications interface between the switch and the controller. Anything "OpenFlow related" happening between the switch and controller—instructions and configuration from the controller to the switch, notifications from the switch to the controller, and packets passing from processing to the controller or from the controller into processing—goes over this channel.

Precedent to connection startup, the switch must be configured with the controller's IP address. Optionally the controller could be configured with the switch's IP address, but the goal is the same: The two devices must be able to find each other.

Channel Connections

The OpenFlow connection operates over TCP, and both the switch and the controller listen on port 6653.[7] The switch initiates the connection to the controller on startup or restart, originating traffic to the default port 6653 or a user-defined port to an ephemeral controller TCP port. Optionally, the switch can allow the controller to initiate the session. Although it can operate "in the clear," the connection is usually encrypted over Transport Layer Security (TLS) Protocol.[8] TLS is similar to, but more secure than, Secure Sockets Layer (SSL). Given the obvious security risks of exposing switches to maliciously "rogue" OpenFlow messages, TLS encryption should always be used.[9]

---

[7] 6653 is the default in Switch Specification 1.3.2 and later. In 1.3.2 and earlier, the default TCP port is 6633, and in some very early versions you might find a default port of 976. The Internet Assigned Numbers Authority (IANA) has assigned TCP port 6653 to OpenFlow, whereas the earlier port numbers were not specifically reserved for this protocol. Therefore you should be aware of these differences if you run 1.3.2 or earlier, but moving forward the default port should remain 6653. You can, of course, change the default port on any version.

[8] T. Dierka and E. Rescorla, "The Transport Layer Security (TLS) Protocol, Version 1.2," RFC 5246, August 2008.

[9] A stand-alone encryption mechanism, such as IPsec, might be used instead of TLS, but that choice is implementation-specific and might hinder interoperability between controllers and switches from different vendors.

Immediately after the TCP session is established and certificates are exchanged by TLS, the controller and switch exchange Hello messages to negotiate the OF version to use. Each side includes in the Hello's version field the highest version of OpenFlow it can support. The highest version that both sides can support is the version that is agreed upon.[10] At this point the connection is up and the controller and switch can exchange messages. The two sides use an Echo Request / Reply process to monitor the connection and the connection latency.

Connection Interruption

If one side cannot support the version advertised by the other side, it sends an error message and the connection is closed. Similarly, if the failure of an established connection is detected either because echo replies are not received, because the TLS session times out, or because of some other evidence of disconnect, the switch will enter one of two states depending on implementation:

- *Fail Secure Mode*: The switch continues to operate, but does not try to send messages or packets to the controller. Entries in the flow tables continue to time out as they normally would.

- *Fail Standalone Mode*: The switch reverts to operating as a standalone (non-OpenFlow) switch. This mode is usually only used by hybrid switches.

A switch also operates in one of these two modes when it first starts and before it establishes a session with a controller. Which mode it uses at startup is implementation-specific, but it can be assumed that OpenFlow-only switches will start in Fail Secure and hybrid switches will start in Fail Standalone.

Connection Reestablishment

When a switch reestablishes a session with the controller after a connection interruption, the existing entries in the flow table continue to be used. The controller can optionally request that the switch send it all flow entries, using a flow stats message, so that the controller can read the entries and synchronize its state to the switch accordingly. The controller also has the option of deleting the switches' flow entries and then synchronizing the switch by sending it a fresh set of flow entries using flow modification messages. Leaving flow entries alone at reestablishment runs the risk of having inaccurate forwarding information, while the latter option disrupts all forwarding until the switch and controller are re-synchronized.

---

[10] Some implementations avoid this negotiation and simply require that the version be configured.

Reliable Message Delivery

The reliability of the OpenFlow message delivery depends on the underlying TCP and TLS mechanisms. It does not use its own acknowledgements of messages, and it does not assume ordered delivery of messages. In fact, the switch can reorder received messages from the controller to optimize performance. For example, a controller might send flow modification messages to the switch in a certain order, but the switch might insert the resulting flow entries into its tables in a different order.

Message Categories

OpenFlow messages between the controller and switch fall into one of three categories:

- *Controller-to-Switch* messages are used by the controller to manage the switch. Using these messages the controller not only can add, modify, or delete flow table entries, but it can also query the switch for features and statistics, configure the switch, set switch port properties, and send packets out a specified switch port.

- *Asynchronous* messages are sent from the switch to the controller. These messages can be a packet or packet header that does not match any flow entry and therefore needs to be processed at the controller, a notification of a change in flow state or port status, or an error message.

- *Symmetric* messages can be sent by either the controller or the switch. These messages are hellos (keepalives), echo requests, and replies, or experimenter messages that enable additional functionality.

The specific messages under each of these types are presented later in the chapter. For now, it is enough to be aware of these message types and how they are exchanged across the secure channel.

Connecting to Multiple Controllers

Redundancy is essential to any reliable network design, and an OpenFlow controller / switch architecture is no exception. Although we mostly focus on the relationship between a single controller and a single switch throughout this chapter, a realistic OpenFlow design connects each switch to multiple controllers to eliminate single points of failure at the controller and at the connection to the controller.

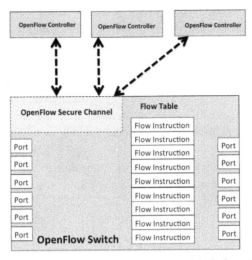

Figure 3.3: An OpenFlow Switch can Connect to Multiple Controllers

How the multiple controllers synchronize with each other is specific to the controller implementation and is not important to OpenFlow. But a switch connecting to multiple controllers must be able to categorize the relationships of the controllers to each other from the switch's perspective. A controller can play one of three roles:

- *Equal* is the default role. The switch exchanges the same messages with each controller, and does not distinguish between them, and does not load-balance among the controllers or arbitrate between the controllers. The switch relies on the controllers to coordinate the instructions they send to the switch.

- *Master* is the same as Equal in terms of the relationship between the switch and controller, but the difference is that only a single controller can be Master. If there is a Master, all other controllers must be in a Slave role because if one controller is in Master state and another controller is in Equal state, there is no mechanism to arbitrate controller permissions at the switch.

- *Slave* is the role of all switches except the Master, when controllers are set up in a Master/Slave configuration. A Slave controller cannot send any Controller-to-Switch messages that would cause a change to the switch; it can only send messages of this type that query information from the switch or that inform the switch of its role. Similarly, a Slave controller cannot receive any Asynchronous messages except Port Status messages.

A switch cannot dictate on its own what role the controller plays. Each controller is responsible for sending a Controller-to-Switch message called Role Request to tell the switch what its role is. Although OpenFlow does not specify the Master/Slave election mechanism between controllers, it does specify a 64-bit number, called *Generation-ID*, in the Role Request message that allows the switch to keep track of the most recent Role Request messages during a role change. This avoids a situation where multiple Slave controllers, during election, might declare themselves Master and the switch does not know who to believe.

A controller can also send Asynchronous Configuration messages to the switch that change default behaviors so that, for example, different notification messages are sent to different controllers.

Auxiliary Connections

Just as you can have a switch connect to more than one controller, you can have multiple connections between the switch and a controller. It's a good idea for the same reason: redundancy. But multiple connections also enable load balancing of messages and can improve overall connection performance between the controller and the switch.

The auxiliary links use the same IP addresses and transport port numbers at each end as the main, but they can use different transport than the main. For instance, the main might use TLS, whereas the auxiliaries might use unencrypted TCP. (Although, because you *can* do this does not mean you *should* do this.)

When there are multiple connections, one connection is the *main* and the others are *auxiliary* connections. The main connection must be established first, and then the auxiliary connections are established. And if the main is torn down, the auxiliaries must also go down. But while they are up, the main and auxiliary connections are treated the same, and all message types can be sent on all connections.

Two identifiers are used with auxiliary connections:

- *Datapath ID* identifies all the connections between the same switch and the same controller. That is, the main and the auxiliaries all use the same Datapath ID.

- *Auxiliary ID* differentiates the main connection from an auxiliary connection. The Auxiliary ID of the main is zero, and the Auxiliary ID of an auxiliary link is some non-zero number.

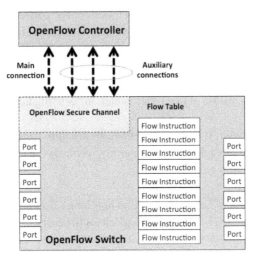

Figure 3.4: A Switch can have More than One Connection to a Controller

Flow Table

The flow table consists of a set of flow entries; each flow entry, as illustrated in Figure 3.5, consists of:

- A *Match* field, specifying the conditions under which a packet is matched. This can be a combination of incoming port, Ethernet and IPv4 header fields, higher-layer ports, or metadata.
- A *Priority* field, used along with the match field, to set the precedence of the flow entry.
- A *Counter* field to record statistics of matching packets.
- An *Instruction* field to specify actions to be performed on matching packets. In early versions of OpenFlow, this field is called Actions.
- A *Timeouts* field to specify the maximum amount of time or idle time before the entry is expired by the switch.
- A *Cookie* field used by the controller to filter flow entries. The data in this field is opaque to the switch, and is not used for packet processing. The cookie field was added in 1.3.0.
- *Flags* used for altering the way flows are managed. Flags were added in 1.3.3.

Figure 3.5: The Flow Eentry Format

There might be multiple flow entries that contain match conditions for a packet; the entry with the most conditions matching the packet is the matching entry, and the actions in that entry's instruction field are followed. The packet might be forwarded out of the switch on a physical or logical port, or it might be forwarded to the controller, flooded, or referred to default switch processing through a Flood or Normal reserved ports.

The timeouts field consists of two timer values, for deleting flow entries:

- *Hard Timeout*, if non-zero, defines an absolute time—regardless of how many matches a flow entry has or how recently the matches occurred—at which the flow entry is deleted.

- *Idle Timeout*, if non-zero, specifies how long a flow entry can exist without having a match before the switch deletes the entry.

While a switch can remove a flow entry based on these timeouts, a controller can actively delete an entry with a *Delete* message.

It's important to note that the flow table in the switch is not the same thing as the Forwarding Information Base (FIB). A FIB is a simple set of forwarding instructions mapping, at a minimum, a destination address to an outgoing port. It supports *destination-based* switching. An OpenFlow flow table is a sequential set of instructions matching multiple fields, and taking some action based on that match—it supports *flow-based* switching. Of course, the match condition in a flow entry could be just a destination address, and the action could be to forward matching packets out port X—just like a FIB. So you might say that a flow table is a superset of a FIB.

This differentiation between OF flow tables and the traditional FIB is also important because OpenFlow switches can be either OpenFlow-only or hybrid, as discussed previously in this chapter. A hybrid switch can run under both an SDN controller and the switch vendor's proprietary control plane. There can even be interaction between the flow tables and the FIB as a packet is forwarded through the hybrid switch.

Some of the flow entry elements, such as cookies and flags, are meaningful only within the smaller details of OpenFlow, and are not discussed further in this chapter. If you want to know more about them, have a look at the relevant switch specifications. Other elements, such as matching and the resulting actions prescribed in the Instructions field, are at the heart of OpenFlow functions and are described in greater detail later in this chapter.

Pipeline

A switch with a single flow table, as we have described it so far, is specified in Switch Specification 1.0.0. The problem with this single-table implementation is that it doesn't scale. Early implementations were built using TCAMs, which were limited to a few thousand entries, and the match criteria only examined 12 fields in the packet headers.[11] When a match occurred, the switch was limited to just seven different actions.

To remedy the limitations of a single-table switch, 1.1.0 introduced multiple tables and a mechanism, called pipeline processing (Figure 3.6), which allowed the user to create a hierarchy of processing options using a sort of "if-then-goto" logic. The OpenFlow pipeline is a series of flow tables, numbered sequentially starting with 0. All incoming packets to the switch must be processed through table 0, and then may be forwarded to some numerically higher table along with *metadata* that can be matched at the next table.

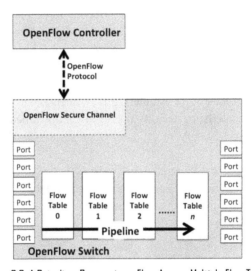

Figure 3.6: A Ppipeline, Processing a Flow Across Multiple Flow Tables

Figure 3.7[12] illustrates how pipeline processing works. When a packet arrives on some port, the ingress port is recorded and the packet is sent to flow table 0 (processing must always begin at flow table 0). An *Action Set* is associated with the flow, which is initially an empty set. If a matching flow entry is found, the associated instructions in that entry are either executed or added to the Action Set. One of the instructions can be a Go-To instruction, which sends the packet to another,

---

[11] Those original twelve match fields were Ingress Port, Ethernet Source MAC address, Ethernet Destination MAC address, Ethertype, VLAN ID VLAN Priority, IPv4 Source address, IPv4 Destination address, IPv4 Protocol Number, IPv4 ToS bits, TCP/UDP Source port, and TCP/UDP Destination port.

[12] Figure 3.7 is based closely on an illustration of pipeline processing in the OpenFlow Switch Specifications.

numerically higher table[13] along with the associated Action Set, metadata (any inter-table information), and the ingress port ID.

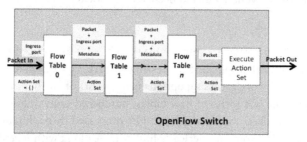

Figure 3.7: Information Shared from Table to Table During Pipeline Processing

The process is repeated at each table, and after the last table in the pipeline has processed the packet, the instructions in the Action Set are executed sequentially.

A *Table-miss* occurs if a packet does not match any flow entry at a given table. The switch has to know what to do with a packet in this event, so the controller should add a Table-miss entry to each flow table. If a Table-miss entry is not included in the table (and they do not exist by default), the default action when no match is found in the table is to drop the packet.

The single pipeline process illustrated in Figure 3.7 is linear. But Figure 3.8 shows how different match conditions can point to different tables, creating a complex series of processing actions.

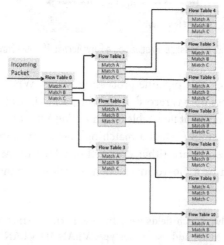

Figure 3.8: Pipelining Enables Complex Hierarchies of Flow Processing

---

[13] A Go-To cannot send a packet to a numerically lower table, causing the processing sequence to run backwards.

Group Table

Switch Specification 1.1.0 also introduced *group tables* (Figure 3.9). Like a flow table, a group table consists of a set of entries—in this case, group entries, each of which represents some group of packets that should be treated in the same way. A group is a means of applying a common set of output actions to aggregate flows; that is, by designating a packet as a member of a group, actions can be efficiently applied or changed across multiple flows. In this way OpenFlow groups are conceptually like MPLS Forward Equivalence Classes (FECs).

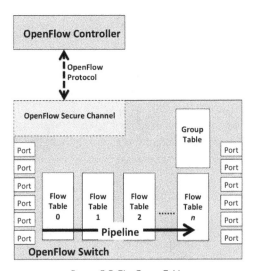

Figure 3.9: The Group Table

Each group entry (Figure 3.10) consists of:

- A 32-bit *group identifier*
- A *group type*, which is one of:
    - *All*: Executes all sets of actions defined for the group. This is used for multicast and broadcast, where the packet is replicated for each action set (action bucket).
    - *Select*: Using a selection algorithm such as round-robin or a hash based on user definitions, the packet is sent to only one of the group's action sets. Multipath load balancing is achieved by this group type.
    - *Indirect*: Executes a single action set for all packets sent to the group. This group type is used for efficiently applying an action set to multiple flows.
    - *Fast Failover*: This group type has an action set associated with an individual port, and executes the first live action set (as determined by a liveness detection mechanism). As the name implies, this group type

allows forwarding to be quickly moved from a failed port to a live port without consulting the controller.

- A *counter* field to record statistics of matching packets.
- *Action buckets,* which each contain a set of actions to be executed; the group's action bucket performs a similar role as the instruction set in a flow entry. As the descriptions of the four group types imply, there are different action buckets for different group types.

Figure 3.10: The Group Entry Format

Meter Table

The last of the OpenFlow components to discuss is the *meter table*, introduced in 1.3.0. A meter table allows OpenFlow to create a simple Quality of Service (QoS) mechanism that measures the rate of a flow and then imposes a specified rate limit. Each entry (Figure 3.11) on the meter table represents a meter. A meter is associated directly with a flow entry[14], and measures the rate of the matching flow.

The fields within the meter entry are as follows:

- *Meter Identifier* is a 32-bit unsigned integer identifying the meter.
- *Meter Bands* is an unordered list of meter bands, each of which specifies a rate and an instruction for processing a packet. A meter can have one or more bands.
- *Counters* are incremented whenever a meter processes a packet.

Figure 3.11: The Meter Entry Format

A meter band (Figure 3.12) consists of the following fields:

- *Band Type* specifies how a packet is to be processed.
- *Rate* specifies the lowest rate at which the meter band can apply.
- *Burst* defines the granularity of the meter band.
- *Counters* are incremented when a packet is processed by the band.
- *Type Specific Arguments* are used with some band types to define additional instructions.

---

[14] A meter is attached to a flow entry when the entry specifies the meter in its instruction set.

Figure 3.12: The Meter Band Format

The OpenFlow Protocol

Now that we've introduced the components of an OpenFlow implementation and have seen how they work together, we can take a closer look at some of the details of those components. In this section, we will take a closer look at the essential OpenFlow messages exchanged between the switch and the controller over the secure channel.

Message Header

All OpenFlow messages are encapsulated with an OpenFlow header, shown in Figure 3.13. The fields are:

- *Version*: The OpenFlow Switch Specification standard to which the message is compliant. The value in this field corresponds to the Wire Protocol Number associated with each version, as shown in Table 3.1. To recap, they are:
    - Version 1.0.0 = 0x01
    - Version 1.1.0 = 0x02
    - Version 1.2 = 0x03
    - Version 1.3.0 = 0x04
    - Version 1.3.1 = 0x04
    - Version 1.3.2 = 0x04
    - Version 1.3.3 = 0x04
    - Version 1.3.4 = 0x04
    - Version 1.4.0 = 0x05
- *Type* is, obviously, the type of message. Table 3.2 lists the message types, along with their general function and which of the general message types they are.
- *Length* indicates the total length of the message.
- *Transaction ID* (XID) is similar to a sequence number; its job is to identify a specific message, so that if multiple messages of the same type are received, a switch or controller can determine which is more recent. Replies to a querying message using a given XID use the same XID, to ensure that they are associated with the correct query.

Version (8 bytes)	Type (8 bytes)	Length (16 bytes)
Transaction Identifier (XID) (32 bytes)		

Figure 3.13: The OpenFlow Message Header

Table 3.2: OpenFlow Message Types

Message	Type Number	Message Category
Immutable Messages		
HELLO	0	Symmetric Message
ERROR	1	Async Message
ECHO REQUEST	2	Symmetric Message
ECHO REPLY	3	Symmetric Message
EXPERIMENTER	4	Symmetric Message
Switch Configuration Messages		
FEATURES REQUEST	6	Controller/Switch Message
FEATURES REPLY	6	Controller/Switch Message
GET CONFIG REQUEST	7	Controller/Switch Message
GET CONFIG REPLY	8	Controller/Switch Message
SET CONFIG	9	Controller/Switch Message
Asynchronous Messages		
PACKET IN	10	Async Message
FLOW REMOVED	11	Async Message
PORT STATUS	12	Async Message
Controller Command Messages		
PACKET OUT	13	Controller/Switch Message
FLOW MOD	14	Controller/Switch Message
GROUP MOD	15	Controller/Switch Message
PORT MOD	16	Controller/Switch Message
TABLE MOD	17	Controller/Switch Message
Multipart Messages		
MULTIPART REQUEST	18	Controller/Switch Message
MULTIPART REPLY	19	Controller/Switch Message

Message	Type Number	Message Category
Barrier Messages		
BARRIER REQUEST	20	Controller/Switch Message
BARRIER REPLY	21	Controller/Switch Message
Queue Configuration Messages		
QUEUE GET CONFIG REQUEST	22	Controller/Switch Message
QUEUE GET CONFIG REPLY	23	Controller/Switch Message
Controller Role Change Request Messages		
ROLE REQUEST	24	Controller/Switch Message
ROLE REPLY	25	Controller/Switch Message
Asynchronous Message Configuration		
GET ASYNC REQUEST	26	Controller/Switch Message
GET ASYNC REPLY	27	Controller/Switch Message
SET ASYNC	28	Controller/Switch Message
Meters and Rate Limiters Configuration Messages		
METER MOD	29	Controller/Switch Message

Message Structures

There are a number of structures that are used within OpenFlow messages to describe functional elements of the switch. These are:

- *Port Structures*, which define physical, logical, and reserved ports. Details of the port include a 32-bit port number, the port type, and port type-dependent characteristics such as port state and port speed for physical ports.
- *Queue Structures*, which describe queues on the output port of the data path. Each queue is described by:
- A 32 bit *port number*
- A 32 bit *queue ID*
- Minimum and maximum rate properties
- *Flow Match* structures, which describe matching packets or flow entries. The match fields are described in the next section, "Flow Processing."

Message Types

The OpenFlow message types are listed in Table 3.2. You have also already seen, earlier in this chapter, that messages fall into one of three categories. Repeating the earlier descriptions, these categories are:

- *Controller-to-Switch* messages, used by the controller to manage the switch. Using these messages the controller not only can add, modify, or delete flow table entries, but it can also query the switch for features and statistics, configure the switch, set switch port properties, and send packets out a specified switch port.

- *Asynchronous* messages, sent from the switch to the controller without any solicitation from the controller. These messages can be a packet or packet header that does not match any flow entry and therefore needs to be processed at the controller, a notification of a change in flow state or port status, or an error message.

- *Symmetric* messages, sent by either the controller or the switch. These messages are hellos (keepalives), echo requests and replies, or experimenter messages that enable additional functionality.

The list of message types in Table 3.2 indicates the category to which each message type belongs. Table 3.3 describes how the message types are used to perform several OpenFlow operations.

Table 3.3: OpenFlow Message Operations

Function	Messages Used	Description
Controller to Switch Messages		
Handshake	FEATURES REQUEST FEATURES REPLY	Identify a switch at startup and describe the switch capabilities
Switch Configuration	GET CONFIG REQUEST GET CONFIG REPLY SET CONFIG	The controller can request configuration information and make configuration changes
Flow Table Configuration	TABLE MOD	Change a flow table configuration
Modify Flow Entry	FLOW MOD	Add, change, or remove flow entries, and specify parameters such as timeouts
Modify Group Entry	GROUP MOD	Add, change, or remove group table entries, and specify parameters such as action buckets

Function	Messages Used	Description
Port Modification	PORT MOD	Modify the behavior of a physical port
Meter Modification	METER MOD	Add, change, or delete a meter from the meter table, and specify parameters such as rate and burst size
Multipart Data Request	MULTIPART REQUEST MULTIPART REPLY	Request data from the switch that might not fit into a single normal OpenFlow message, which is limited in size to 64 KB, such as flow, queue or port statistics or switch manufacturer information
Queue Configuration	QUEUE GET CONFIG REQUEST QUEUE GET CONFIG REPLY	Request queue information[15]
Packet Send	PACKET OUT	Send a packet out through the datapath
Barrier	BARRIER REQUEST BARRIER REPLY	Controller requests notifications about completed operations or ensures dependencies
Role Change	ROLE REQUEST ROLE REPLY	The controller notifies the switch of its role (Equal, Master, or Slave) or a change in its role
Set Asynchronous Configuration	GET ASYNC REQUEST GET ASYNC REPLY SET ASYNC	The controller specifies the asynchronous messages it wants to receive, other than error notifications, or queries for current asynchronous messages it will be sent

---

[15] Switch queues are configured separately from OpenFlow, so a controller can only request information; it cannot change the queue.

Function	Messages Used	Description
Asynchronous Messages		
Packet In	PACKET IN	The switch sends a received packet to the controller, and specifies the reason the packet is being sent (such as no flow match or invalid TTL)
Flow Removed	FLOW REMOVED	Switch notifies the controller that a flow entry has been removed due to timeout or some other reason
Port Status	PORT STATUS	Switch notifies the controller that a port has been added, removed, or changed
Error	ERROR	The switch notifies the controller of a problem and provides information about the nature of the problem
Symmetric Messages		
Hello	HELLO	Used during version negotiation, and as a keepalive
Echo	ECHO REQUEST ECHO REPLY	A "ping" mechanism used for such things as latency or bandwidth measurement
Experimenter	EXPERIMENTER	A message with undefined content that can be used by experimenters

Flow Processing

The heart of OpenFlow, of course, is the processing and switching of data flows. All of the descriptions of basic components, messaging, and functions that we've covered so far have been to get us here, where we can describe how flows are processed in an OpenFlow switch. You have already seen a description of the fields in a flow entry; here we focus on what match criteria are supported in OpenFlow, what is traced with counters, and what actions an OpenFlow switch can perform when a match occurs.

Earlier in this chapter we cautioned that a flow table is not the same thing as a FIB. Although it can do simple matching and forwarding like a FIB, it can do much more than that. The closest comparison to a flow table might be (in Cisco IOS parlance) an access list (ACL) or route map. It is a list of one or more entries, and each entry has a match condition, an action to take on any packets that match, and possibly an accounting function to count how many matches have occurred. The list of flow entries making up a flow table, or multiple flow tables tied together in a pipeline, comprise flow processing.

Match Parameters

OpenFlow match structures are built using a Type/Length/Value (TLV) format, which makes changing or expanding match parameters between versions much easier. In this section we describe the parameters that can be matched as of version 1.3.4. If you are using a different version of OpenFlow, you should consult the relevant specification to see if the parameters discussed here are supported or if additional match parameters are supported.

OpenFlow match conditions fall into one of three categories:

- Flow Match
- Header Match
- Pipeline Match
- Experimenter Flow Match

Flow Match

A flow is usually identified by a combination of parameters such as incoming port, L2 and L3 source and destination addresses, Class of Service (CoS) bits, and upper layer ports. Table 3.4 lists all of the parameters that can be used to specify a flow match.

Table 3.3: Flow Match Fields

Field	Description
IN_PORT	Switch input port
IN_PHY_PORT	Switch physical input port
METADATA	Metadata passed between tables
ETH_DEST	Ethernet destination address
ETH_SRC	Ethernet source address
ETH_TYPE	Ethernet frame type

Field	Description
VLAN_VID	VLAN ID
VLAN_PCP	VLAN priority
IP_DSCP	IP DSCP (6 bits in ToS field)
IP_ECN	IP ECN (2 bits in ToS field)
IP_PROTO	IP protocol number
IPV4_SRC	IPv4 source address
IPV4_DST	IPv4 destination address
TCP_SRC	TCP source port
TCP_DST	TCP destination port
UDP_SRC	UDP source port
UDP_DST	UDP destination port
SCTP_SRC	SCTP source port
SCTP_DST	SCTP destination port
ICMPV4_TYPE	ICMP type
ICMPV4_CODE	ICMP code
ARP_OP	ARP opcode
ARP_SPA	ARP source IPv4 address
ARP_TPA	ARP target IPv4 address
ARP_SHA	ARP source hardware address
ARP_THA	ARP target hardware address
IPV6_SRC	IPv6 source address
IPV6_DST	IPv6 destination address
IPV6_FLABEL	IPv6 Flow Label
ICMPV6_TYPE	ICMPv6 type
ICMPV6_CODE	ICMPv6 code
IPV6_ND_TARGET	IPv6 Neighbor Discovery (ND) target address
IPV6_ND_SLL	IPv6 source link-layer address for ND
IPV6_ND_TLL	IPv6 target link layer address for ND
MPLS_LABEL	MPLS label
MPLS_TC	MPLS traffic class
MPLS_BOS	MPLS Bottom of Stack bit
PBB_ISID	Provider Backbone Bridge (PBB) Service Instance Identifier
TUNNEL_ID	Logical port metadata

Field	Description
IPV6_EXTHDR	IPv6 extension header pseudo-field

Header Match

In addition to flows, a flow entry can match specific packets based on the contents of its Layer 2, 3, and 4 headers. Table 3.4 lists the header fields that can be matched. You can readily see that this is almost the same list as Table 3.3, but without packet-independent parameters such as ingress port, metadata, or tunnel IDs.

Table 3.4: Header Match Fields

Field	Description
ETH_DEST	Ethernet destination address
ETH_SRC	Ethernet source address
ETH_TYPE	Ethernet frame type
VLAN_VID	VLAN ID
VLAN_PCP	VLAN priority
IP_DSCP	IP DSCP (6 bits in ToS field)
IP_ECN	IP ECN (2 bits in ToS field)
IP_PROTO	IP protocol number
IPV4_SRC	IPv4 source address
IPV4_DST	IPv4 destination address
TCP_SRC	TCP source port
TCP_DST	TCP destination port
UDP_SRC	UDP source port
UDP_DST	UDP destination port
SCTP_SRC	SCTP source port
SCTP_DST	SCTP destination port
ICMPV4_TYPE	ICMP type
ICMPV4_CODE	ICMP code
ARP_OP	ARP opcode
ARP_SPA	ARP source IPv4 address
ARP_TPA	ARP target IPv4 address
ARP_SHA	ARP source hardware address
ARP_THA	ARP target hardware address

Field	Description
IPV6_SRC	IPv6 source address
IPV6_DST	IPv6 destination address
IPV6_FLABEL	IPv6 Flow Label
ICMPV6_TYPE	ICMPv6 type
ICMPV6_CODE	ICMPv6 code
IPV6_ND_TARGET	IPv6 Neighbor Discovery (ND) target address
IPV6_ND_SLL	IPv6 source link layer address for ND
IPV6_ND_TLL	IPv6 target link layer address for ND
MPLS_LABEL	MPLS label
MPLS_TC	MPLS traffic class
MPLS_BOS	MPLS Bottom of Stack bit
PBB_ISID	Provider Backbone Bridge (PBB) Service Instance Identifier
IPV6_EXTHDR	IPv6 extension header pseudo-field

Pipeline Match

Pipeline match fields are the information attached to a packet, other than the packet header, for pipeline processing. These parameters are listed in Table 3.5. Notice that they are the fields in Table 3.3 that are not included in Table 3.4.

Table 3.5: Pipeline Match Fields

Field	Description
IN_PORT	Switch input port
IN_PHY_PORT	Switch physical input port
METADATA	Metadata passed between tables
TUNNEL_ID	Logical port metadata

Experimenter Flow Match

Experimenter Flow Match is an optional category that, as you might guess, supports experimentation. The match parameters in this category are defined by the experimenter, not by OpenFlow, and so there are no specifics to describe here.

Instructions and Actions

When a match is found, things start happening. This is also where some OpenFlow terminology can get confusing. There are six concepts you need to be familiar with here: Instructions, Instruction Sets, Actions, Action Lists, Action Sets, and Action Buckets.

There are intertwined dependencies among these six concepts that make defining them a bit of a chicken-and-egg problem: It's hard to completely define instructions without knowing what actions are, and it's hard to completely describe actions without knowing what instructions are. Then there are those lists and sets and buckets to muddy the waters even more. So let's start with a high-level overview of how Instructions, Instruction Sets, Actions, and Action Lists relate to each other. We can then take a closer look at each.

You already know that an individual flow table consists of multiple flow entries, and that an individual flow entry consists of, among other fields, a set of match criteria and one or more Instructions to be executed when a match occurs. As illustrated in Figure 3.14, this set of one or more Instructions in a flow entry is an *Instruction Set*. An individual Instruction in the Instruction Set might or might not have a list of actions—an *Action List*—associated with it. An Action List, as you can easily infer, is a list of one or more individual Actions.

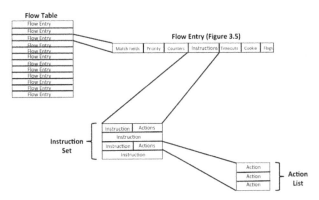

Figure 3.14: The Relationship of Instructions, an Instruction Set, Actions, and an Action List

Recall from Figure 3.7 that an Action Set is passed between flow tables during flow processing. An Action List, on the other hand, is associated with an Instruction within a flow entry of a single flow table.

Instructions

There are six types of instructions, listed in Table 3.6. Some instruction types have actions associated with them, and others do not, but all instructions cause a change of some type—to a packet, an action set, or to pipeline processing. Also some instruction types are required, while others are optional; Table 3.6 indicates which, as of 1.3.4 and 1.4.0. A controller can query a switch to discover which, if any, optional instructions the switch supports.

If a switch cannot execute an instruction in a flow entry given to it by a controller, it rejects the flow entry and sends an error message to the controller.

Table 3.6: Instruction Types

Instruction	Required / Optional	Description
Write-Actions *action(s)*	Required	Adds the specified Action List into the Action Set. If one of the specified actions already exists in the Action Set, overwrite it.
Apply-Actions *action(s)*	Optional	Executes the specified Action List immediately, without changing the Action Set.
Clear-Actions	Optional	Clears all actions in the Action Set immediately.
Goto-Table *next-table-id*	Required	Indicates the Table ID of the next table in the processing pipeline. A matching flow entry without a Goto-Table Instruction indicates the end of the pipeline, and the Action Set is executed.
Meter *meter-id*	Optional	Sends the packet to the specified Meter.
Write-Metadata *metadata / mask*	Optional	Writes the masked metadata value into the metadata field for pipeline processing.

Instruction Sets

An Instruction Set comprises the "Instructions" field in a flow entry (Figure 3.5), and consists of one or more individual Instructions. An individual Instruction Set can only contain one Instruction of each type. For example, an instruction set can contain an Apply-Actions instruction, a Write-Actions instruction, and a Goto-Table instruction, but cannot contain two different Goto-Table instructions. And since there are only six Instruction types (Table 3.6), an Instruction Set can never contain more than six Instructions.

Although a given Instruction Set might not contain Instructions of all six types, Instructions in the set are executed in the following order:

1. Meter
2. Apply-Actions
3. Clear-Actions
4. Write-Actions
5. Write-Metadata
6. Goto-Table

In makes sense that only one Instruction of each type can appear in a given Instruction Set, because you should not be able to send a single matching packet to more than one downstream table in a pipeline, or to more than one meter, or associate more than one metadata value with the packet. If you need to clear an Action Set in the pipeline, you only need to do it once for any matching packet. And if you need to execute multiple Actions or write multiple Actions to an Action Set, you can associate multiple Actions in a single Action list for each of those Instructions.

Action Lists

An Action List consists of one or more individual actions, and is associated with either an Apply-Actions instruction or a Write-Actions instruction. Although not discussed elsewhere in this chapter, the PACKET OUT message (Table 3.2) also has an associated Action List.

- The Apply-Actions instruction immediately executes the actions in the Action List. The actions are executed consecutively, in the order they appear on the list, so the order of the actions can matter. Execution of the actions can change the matched packet in some way, but does not change the Action Set associated with the packet for pipeline processing.

- The Write-Actions instruction writes the actions on the Action List to the Action Set, used on pipeline processing. The actions on the list are not executed by this instruction. If the Action List contains an action that already exists in the Action Set, the action in the Action Set is overwritten.

- The controller uses the PACKET OUT message to send a packet into the switch's dataflow. It can contain an Action List that instructs the switch to modify the packet in some way or to send the packet to a group or to an output port.

Actions

Like Instructions, a switch is required to support certain Actions while support of others is optional. Table 3.7 lists the Action types in current use, and indicates whether they are required or optional. The Action format includes a header that specifies the Action type number, and a length. Note that Table 3.7 indicates only some of the variables that can be specified by an action. For example, the OUTPUT action specifies not only the output port, but can also specify the amount of the packet – from zero to the full length—to be forwarded.

Table 3.7: Action Types

Action	Type	Required / Optional	Description
OUTPUT *port*	0	Required	Forward the packet to a specified OpenFlow port (physical, logical, or reserved). The port is represented by a 32-bit number.
COPY_TTL_OUT	11	Optional	Copy the value of the TTL field in the next-to-outermost header to the TTL field outermost header. No argument is required with this action. The copy can be IP-to-IP, MPLS-to-MPLS, or IP-to-MPLS.
COPY_TTL_IN	12	Optional	Copy the value of the TTL field in the outermost header to the TTL field next-to-outermost header. No argument is required with this action. The copy can be IP-to-IP, MPLS-to-MPLS, or MPLS-to-IP.
SET_MPLS_TTL *mpls_ttl*	15	Optional	Change the value of the TTL field in the outermost MPLS header to the specified value.
DEC_MPLS_TTL	16	Optional	Decrement the value of the TTL field in the outermost MPLS header. There is no argument for this action; the existing TTL value is merely decremented by 1.

Action	Type	Required / Optional	Description
PUSH_VLAN *ethertype*	17	Optional	Push a new VLAN header (C-TAG or S-TAG) into the packet. If a VLAN header already exists, the pushed VLAN tag becomes the outermost tag. The Ethertype field must be either 0x8100 or 0x88a8.
POP_VLAN	18	Optional	Pop the outermost VLAN header from the packet.
PUSH_MPLS *ethertype*	19	Optional	Push a new MPLS shim header into the packet. If an MPLS header already exists, the pushed MPLS label becomes the outermost label. The Ethertype field must be either 0x8847 or 0x8848.
POP_MPLS	20	Optional	Pop the outermost MPLS label or shim header from the packet.
SET_QUEUE *queue_id*	21	Optional	Map the packet to the specified port queue, regardless of the value of the IP DSCP or VLAN PCP bits. Do not change the values of these bits.
GROUP *group_id*	22	Required	Process the packet in the specified group.
SET_NW_TTL *ip_ttl*	23	Optional	Change the value of the IPv4 TTL field or the IPv6 Hop Limit field to the specified value, and updates the IP checksum accordingly.
DEC_NW_TTL	24	Optional	Decrement the value of the IPv4 TTL field or the IPv6 Hop Limit field, and updates the IP checksum accordingly. There is no argument for this action; the existing TTL value is merely decremented by 1.

Action	Type	Required / Optional	Description
SET_FIELD *tlv*	25	Optional	Overwrite a field in the packet to a value specified in the Type / Length / Value (TLV) expression. The field can be any of the fields listed in Table 3.4. The action applies to the outermost header, if there are multiple headers. The header CRC value is recalculated if applicable.
PUSH_PBB *ethertype*	26	Optional	Push a new PBB Service Instance header (I-TAG TCI) onto the packet, and copies the customer addresses (C-DA and C-SA) in the Ethernet addresses of the packet. The Ethertype field must be 0x88e7.
POP_PBB	27	Optional	Pop the outermost PBB Service Instance header from the packet.
EXPERIMENTER *experimenter_id*	0xffff	Optional	Experimental actions
DROP	N/A	Required	DROP is not an explicit or specified action. Rather, it is a default action taken when an Instruction Set or Action Bucket is empty.

An Action List can include multiple PUSH or POP (VLAN, MPLS, or PBB) actions, to add or remove multiple tags. It can also contain multiple SET_FIELD actions when multiple fields are to be modified.

Action Sets

As previously explained (Figure 3.7), an Action Set is used in pipeline processing. An incoming packet has an empty Action Set attached to it, and as the packet is processed across one or more flow tables, matching flow entries use Write-Actions instructions to add actions to the Action Set or Clear-Actions instructions to delete actions from the set. After the last flow table on the pipeline has processed the packet, the actions in the Action Set are executed. Recall that the last flow table on the pipeline is indicated by a matching flow entry that does not have a Goto-Table instruction on its Instruction Set.

Unlike Action Lists, in which multiple actions of the same type can appear (such as multiple PUSH or POP actions to work with stacked tags), an Action Set can contain only one action of each type. The exception to this rule is the SET_FIELD action; the Action Set can contain one SET_FIELD action for each field type (Table 3.4). If an instruction writes an action to an Action Set that already includes an action of that type, the action in the Action Set is overwritten. If multiple actions of the same type need to be executed, the Apply-Actions instruction within a flow entry must be used.

Actions in the Action Set must be executed in the following order:

1. COPY_TTL_IN
2. POP (all tags)
3. PUSH_MPLS
4. PUSH_PBB
5. PUSH_VLAN
6. COPY_TTL_OUT
7. DEC_TTL (all TTL types)
8. SET (all field types)
9. SET_QUEUE
10. GROUP
11. OUTPUT

The actions are executed in this order regardless of the order in which they are added to the Action Set. If there is a requirement for actions to be executed in a different order than this, the Apply-Actions instruction within a flow entry must be used.

Also note that a GROUP action comes before an OUTPUT action. If an Action Set contains both actions, the GROUP action is executed—the packet is set to the specified group—and the OUTPUT action is ignored. If there is neither a GROUP nor an OUTPUT action, or there is no GROUP action and an OUTPUT action points to a non-existent port, the packet is dropped.

Action Buckets

Where an Action Set contains one or more actions, an Action Bucket contains one or more Action Sets. Confused yet? You needn't be. Just think of Actions, Actions Sets, and Action Buckets as a hierarchy: a set of actions, and a set of sets.

Action Buckets, as you already know, are associated with groups. They consist of the Action Sets of the various packets set to a given group, and a matching Group Entry (Figure 3.10) specifies one or more Action Buckets to be executed.

Counters

OpenFlow maintains multiple counters, some required and some optional, for each:

- Flow Table
- Flow Entry
- Port
- Queue
- Group
- Group Bucket
- Meter
- Meter Band

Table 3.8 lists the counters used for each of these entities, the size in bits of each counter, and whether the counter is required or optional. The counters wrap when they exceed the maximum bits, and there is no overflow indicator.

Note that each flow entry, port, group queue, and meter has a Duration counter that tracks the amount of time the entity has been installed in the switch. The switch is required to track the duration in seconds, and it can optionally track them in nanoseconds.

Table 3.8: OpenFlow Counters

Counter	Bits	Required / Optional
Per Flow Table		
Reference Count (active entries)	32	Required
Packet Lookups	64	Optional
Packet Matches	64	Optional
Per Flow Entry		
Received Packets	64	Optional
Received Bytes	64	Optional
Duration (seconds)	32	Required
Duration (nanoseconds)	32	Optional
Per Port		
Received Packets	64	Required
Transmitted Packets	64	Required
Received Bytes	64	Optional

Counter	Bits	Required / Optional
Transmitted Bytes	64	Optional
Receive Drops	64	Optional
Transmit Drops	64	Optional
Receive Errors	64	Optional
Transmit Errors	64	Optional
Receive Frame Alignment Errors	64	Optional
Receive Overrun Errors	64	Optional
Receive CRC Errors	64	Optional
Collisions	64	Optional
Duration (seconds)	32	Required
Duration (nanoseconds)	32	Optional
Per Queue		
Transmit Packets	64	Required
Transmit Bytes	64	Optional
Transmit Overrun Errors	64	Optional
Duration (seconds)	32	Required
Duration (nanoseconds)	32	Optional
Per Group		
Reference Count (flow entries)	32	Optional
Packet Count	64	Optional
Byte Count	64	Optional
Duration (seconds)	32	Required
Duration (nanoseconds)	32	Optional
Per Group Bucket		
Packet Count	32	Optional
Byte Count	64	Optional
Per Meter		
Flow Count	32	Optional
Input Packet Count	64	Optional
Input Byte Count	64	Optional
Duration (seconds)	32	Required
Duration (nanoseconds)	32	Optional

Counter	Bits	Required / Optional
Per Meter Band		
In Band Packet Count	64	Optional
In Band Byte Count	64	Optional

Conclusion

This chapter provides you with a mid-level view into the operation of OpenFlow, but it is not by any means a deep examination. For instance, if you are debugging a message flow and want to know what all the fields in a message mean, you'll need to delve into the relevant OpenFlow Switch Specification document. Here, we have endeavored only to give you an understanding of how OpenFlow works without burying you in esoteric details.

4

OpenFlow in Action

This chapter looks at OpenFlow in action. At the time of this writing, several products support OpenFlow, both on a commercial level and an open source level. The good news is that if you want to learn or test OpenFlow, there are several options. In this chapter we will look at using Mininet with OpenFlow as well as a few commercial options.

OpenFlow Products

Commercial Products

Everyday more and more products are supporting OpenFlow. It is important, however, to examine which version of OpenFlow the products support. Many products claim to support OpenFlow, but when digging a bit deeper, it is discovered that only OpenFlow 1.0 is supported. Although OpenFlow 1.0 is a good version to learn and test OpenFlow concepts due to its single table limitations, it does not scale well and it is not considered deployable.

Listing all the commercial products that support OpenFlow today would be almost impossible, as the product support changes daily. Although there are more vendors everyday that support OpenFlow, here is a short list of some of the early adoptors:

- Alcatel-Lucent / Nuage Networks – Virtualized Services Platform (VSP)
- Big Switch Networks – Switch Light
- Brocade
- Centec Network

- Cisco Systems
- Extreme Networks
- HP
- IBM
- Juniper Networks
- NEC
- Noviflow
- PICA8

As discussed in the previous chapter an OpenFlow network you need to have a controller that is pushing down the OpenFlow rules to the forwarding devices. So many of the vendors listed above have both switches (forwarding elements) as well as controllers. Of course with true OpenFlow interoperability, any controller that speaks OpenFlow should be able to be used.

Open Source Switching Products

What are your options if you want to go the open source route? Well again, this changes quite often but the most common switch is Open vSwitch (OVS). This is popular since it now ships as part of the standard Linux distribution in the Apache 2 license. OVS is a true software switch implemented in the kernel of Linux. It supports OpenFlow as well as many other features you would expect on a switch such as VLANs and link aggregation.

Open vSwitch can operate both as a softswitch running within the hypervisor, and as the control stack for switching silicon. Many bare metal and whitebox vendors have based their product on Open vSwitch.

A Brief History of OVS

Where did OVS come from? From all history reports it spawned from Ethane in 2007 and was called Vigilante at the time and written in C++. (See chapter 2 for more info on Ethane).

OpenFlow appeared in 2008 and new names were formed such as firefly, enso, and Viros. Around 2007 Martin Casado, Nick McKeown and Scott Shenker formed Nicira who ended up taking the code and converting it mostly into C.

By 2009 significant work had been done on OVS and a protocol called OVSDB was developed in order to remotely configure the software switch. By 2010 OpenFlow 1.0 was officially placed into OVS.

OVS continues to have contributors from a variety of sources including Nicira/VMware, who now also maintain a commercial version.

Another open source switch project is called Indigo, which is part of the Floodlight open source project. Indigo is currently the base of Big Switch's Switchlight product; however, the open source version can be used as part of the Eclipse Public License. This software switch is Linux-compatible with the KVM hypervisor. Although not as popular as OVS this may be a good option when looking at using and testing OpenFlow.

Open Source Controller Products

Once you decide on your softswitch you must also pick a controller to interface with your OpenFlow forwarding devices. There are many options in the open source world, depending on what you are trying to accomplish. The two most widely used are Open Daylight (ODL) and Floodlight., although in recent time Open Daylight has taken the clear lead on development time, commercial products and mind share. Open Daylight was discussed in previous chapters, and Floodlight was based on the original OpenFlow controllers from the Clean Slate program. Both of these open source controllers provide a basis for many other vendors' commercial controllers.

Below is a list of the most popular open source controllers on the market today.

Table 1. Open Source Controllers

Vendor	Controllers
Open Daylight	Linux foundation group, Hydrogen, is the first simultaneous release of OpenDaylight delivering three different editions to help a wide array of users get up and running as quickly as possible--Base Edition, Virtualization Edition, and Service Provider Edition.
Floodlight	Enterprise-class, Apache-licensed, Java-based OpenFlow Controller, the alternative to Open Daylight for commercial vendors base code
Ryu	Ryu is a component-based software-defined networking framework based on Python
POX	Young sibling of NOX. Primary target is research. Python-based
NOX	NOX is the original OpenFlow controller, and facilitates development of fast C++ controllers on Linux.

Trema	Trema is a full-stack, easy-to-use framework for developing OpenFlow controllers in Ruby and C
Beacon	Beacon is a fast, cross-platform, modular, Java-based OpenFlow controller that supports both Event-based and threaded operation.
ovs–controller	Trivial reference controller packaged with Open vSwitch.

Testing OpenFlow with Mininet

One of the easiest ways to test OpenFlow is to use a tool called Mininet. Mininet is a network emulator that allows you to create hosts, switches, routers, and links. It can easily run on your laptop, a server, a VM, or in the cloud and allows pre-built and custom topologies to be created in just a few seconds.

The other nice feature of Mininet is that you can install different programs to interact with Mininet, such as Wireshark, which allows you to take packet captures of all inter-link communications.

Introduction to Mininet

The easiest way to get started is to download a pre-packaged Mininet file from http://mininet.org/download/. You also have options to do native installations into Ubuntu. In the Mininet pre-package, however, you get all the OpenFlow binaries and tools such as Wireshark pre-installed.

As previously mentioned you can run Mininet on a variety of platforms; however, one of the simplest methods is to run a virtualization program such as VMware's workstation, or run it freely on VirtualBox. (My preferred method due to the zero cost and easy set-up).

The first thing you need to do when you launch Mininet is to build a topology using a topo command. There are several different "pre-canned" topologies in Mininet that you can use but you can also build them yourself. We will use a few of them in the examples below. Here are a few quick commands:

- sudo mn –topo minimal (creates 2 hosts and 1 switch)
- sudo mn –topo linear, n minimal (creates 1 switch to connect to each host, and all switches are connected together)
- sudo mn –topo single, n minimal (creates 1 switch and n hosts)
- sudo mn –topo tree, depth=n, fanout=n (tree-based topology)

Once you are in Mininet there are several commands you can run to test things. Here are some of the most useful:

- help - displays all CLI commands
- nodes - displays nodes
- net - displays links
- -n ifconfig -displays interface configuration, for example s1 ifconfig
- Ping -packet internet groper

Mininet Example with Floodlight

In this example we will use Mininet with a Floodlight controller. It is important to load a controller into Mininet to avoid using the default reference controller (which acts like a hub.)

First we start the Floodlight controller:

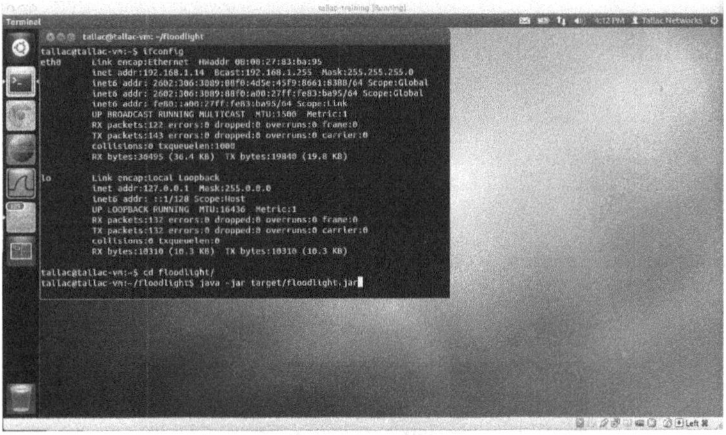

Figure 1. Floodlight Controller Start

A linear topology is created with two switches and two hosts.

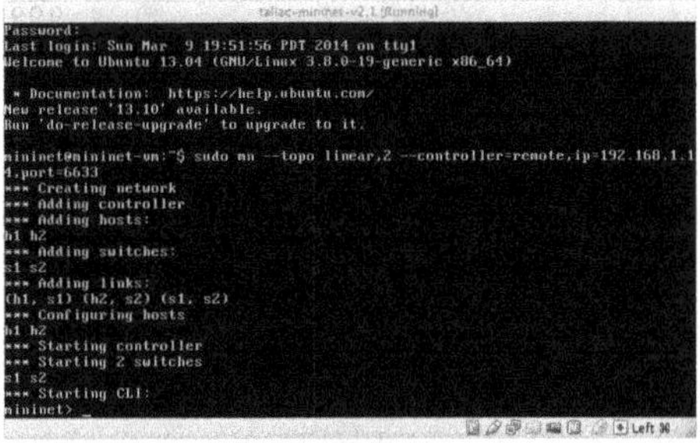

Figure 2. Mininet Topology

The Floodlight controller has a GUI that is used to verify it sees the topology that was created. As you can see from the figure, two hosts and two switches are created.

Figure 3. Floodlight GUI

Let's go ahead and generate some traffic between hosts to verify connectivity just in case.

Figure 4. SDN Host Ping

Going back to the GUI you can see that flows are being created on the controllers. In this configuration on floodlight the controller acts like a "learning bridge" to satisfy basic connectivity. Recall from previous chapters that if there is no rule associated with a received packet, the packet is sent up to the controller. This allows the controller to see MAC addresses and "learn" where hosts are located. After the first packet, the flow rules are sent down to the switches and the controller is only tracking the flows and not involved in packet forwarding.

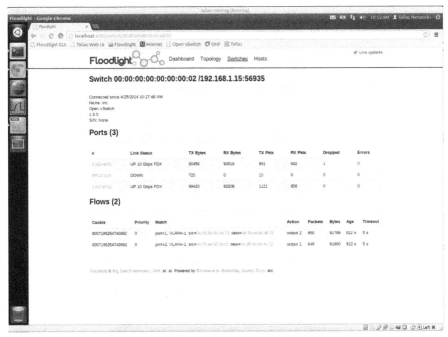

Figure 5. Floodlight Results

You can also see these flows in the Mininet Command Line Interface (CLI) by using a command called ovs-ofctl dump flows. The ovs-ofctl is an OVS command that monitors and configures the switch. There are various options that can be used with the ovs-ofctl command. In this case we are using the dump option to dump flow information. We can see switch 1 by looking at port 6633 and switch 2 by looking at port 6634.

When looking at the flow you see the following info in the entry:

- Cookie - opaque data field used by controller
- Duration - Current time flow has been alive
- Table - the index of the table read. In this case OpenFlow 1.0 is using a single table
- n_packets - number of packets on flow
- n_bytes - number of bytes on flow
- idle_timeout - idle time before flow expires (default 5 seconds)
- idle_age - current age of flow
- priority - priority of flow rule
- in_port - incoming port

- vlan-tci - vlan tag if any
- dl_src - source mac
- dl_dst - destination MAC
- actions - actions, which in the flow entries below, indicate to forward out a given port

Figure 6. OpenFlow Table Output

Of course it would not be too exciting to just use the default behavior, so you can start to write very basic rules to make new flow entries. Here is an example of a very simple source and destination drop rule using the ovs-ctl command.

Figure 7. Manual OpenFlow Rules

What about all this RESTful API stuff?

Of course one of the most significant topics about SDN is the ability to program your network with a series of APIs. One of the most talked about API is the RESTful API, which allows you to make calls to a device using "web-like" languages and calls. At first API's may seem like a bunch of gibberish but you can n play around with a RESTful API in Mininet with the Floodlight controller.

There are a few ways to interface with the RESTful API but one of the basic and most manual ways if the use of *curl* commands. A *curl* command is a way to get data from a device using a variety of protocols such as HTTP, which allows you to interface with a RESTful API. For example, here is a curl command that sets the same rule we saw from the CLI in the above example:

Figure 8. API Rule

The –d option pushes the http message in the JSON format over to the controller.

You can also pull data using the API such as flow rules. Notice the blank action in the output below, which indicates a drop condition.

Figure 9. API Call Flow Output

Mininet Example with Open Daylight

Of course using Mininet you can load any controller you wish including the ever popular Open Daylight. Here is a capture of the ODL controller using the same two switch and two host topology as Floodlight.

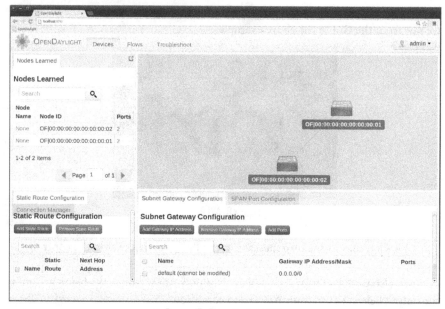

Figure 10. Open Daylight GUI

You can run through the same exercises as the Floodlight controller and start to examine the differences from one controller to another.

A Difference in Defaults

By default, the OpenDaylight controller does not have a "learning switch" functionality. It is enabled by default to perform reactive forwarding (this can be verified by clicking on the "Node" option in the "Nodes Learned" window). What this means is that by default the controller will detect IP packets and flood them out all ports. It learns the source MAC address of the packets coming in on a port. It is not configured to flood ARP frames, and hence, when testing initial ping tests will fail. Most people write static flow entries to change this behavior.

Mininet Example with HP VAN controller

Without getting too redundant when we say that any controller could be used with the Mininet topology we mean even commercial controllers! Here is a snapshot of a controller produced by HP called the VAN controller.

Figure 11. HP VAN GUI

Obviously, to use a commercial controller like HP you must acquire a license for its use.

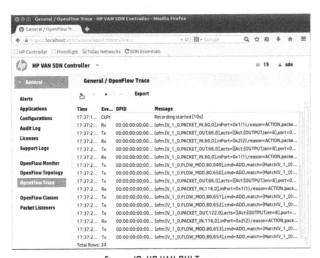

Figure 12. HP VAN GUI Trace

Testing OpenFlow with Hardware

You can also test OpenFlow on physical hardware as well. As mentioned at the beginning of the chapter multiple vendors support controllers and switches with OpenFlow. Each vendor will have their own unique features and licensing requirements. Just remember to always look at the OpenFlow version the vendor claims to support and test, test, test away to make sure there is true interoperability.

NEC Example

We will show one example of a small system sold by a vendor called NEC. NEC's controller heavily uses a concept they called Virtual Tenant Network (VTN). In fact VTNs were submitted as an Open Daylight project and also found their way into the ODL open source controller. I do want to give some credit for this example to engineer at SDN Essentials, Darien Hirotsu who's blog was the basis for this section!

A VTN is a technology to create virtual networks on top of OpenFlow-based packet forwarding hardware. This allows you to design and deploy virtual networks using the controller and OpenFlow as the southbound protocol, which allows users to design and deploy any desired network without knowing the physical network topology or bandwidth restrictions. VTN allows the users to define the network with a look and feel of conventional L2/L3 network. Once the network is designed on VTN, it will automatically be mapped into the underlying physical network, and then configured on the individual switch leveraging OpenFlow. The definition of a logical plane makes it possible not only to hide the complexity of the underlying network but also to better manage network resources. It achieves reducing reconfiguration time of network services and minimizing network configuration errors.

VTNs may seem a little abstract at first but let's look at a very basic topology where we are trying to provide connectivity and isolation for two tenants, VM1 and VM2 which are part of that same VTN. ReIn this case we are using NEC's PFC6800 as the controller and PF5240 as the OpenFlow switch. We are using a separate control network to connect the controller and the switch.

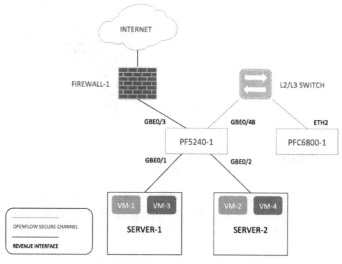

Figure 13. Sample Topology

Here is our default flow table on our programmable flow switch. The switch is installing a flow for each interface with a physical link. The action for each flow is to redirect the frame to the controller.

```
PF5240-1# show openflow table
Date 2000/03/02 19:08:43 UTC


[OpenFlow 1]

  <pri>    <in port>  <entry no> <matched octets> <matched packets><table>
  23000       any       4026          0                  0            nm2
* 2 0/01 [0x00000001]   4027         5618                53           nm2
* 2 0/02 [0x00000002]   4028          0                  0            nm2
* 2 0/03 [0x00000003]   4029          0                  0            nm2
* 2 0/04 [0x00000004]   4030          0                  0            nm2

PF5240-1# show openflow table detail 4027 detail
Date 2000/03/02 19:08:01 UTC


[OpenFlow 1]

<entry 4027>
  table type                 : normal2
  forwarding state           : software-based
  matched octets             : 1272
  matched packets            : 12
  green and yellow octets    : 1166
  green and yellow packets   : 11
  red octets                 : 0
  red packets                : 0
  idle timer(max/current)    : 0 sec / 0 sec
  hard timer(max/current)    : 0 sec / 0 sec
  priority                   : 2
  added command              : pf flowmod
  flow flags                 : SEND_PF_FLOW_REM
  added time                 : 2000/03/02 19:07:43 UTC
  last modified time         : -
  flow cookie                : 0x0

match
  match type                 : VENDOR
  input port                 : 0/01 [0x00000001]
  metadata                   : 0x0000000000000000
  src mac address            : any
  dst mac address            : any
  input vlan                 : any
  input vlan pcp             : any
  ethernet type              : any

action 1
  type                       : OUTPUT
  out port                   : CONTROLLER
  max length                 : NO_BUFFER
  packet_in reason           : ACTION
```

Note that flow entry 4027 above meets the OpenFlow Switch Specification 1.0 that states:

```
"If no match is found, the packet is forwarded to the controller over the
secure channel."
```

Now, since we want to create a basic bridged network, we need to configure a VTN with a vbridge and two vexternal hosts. Vbridge and vexternal is the NEC verbiage, meaning we are creating a virtual Layer 2 switch that will bridge Ethernet frames between two devices.

Here is the VTN topology:

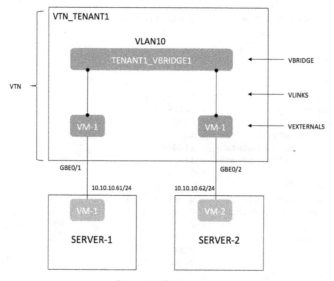

Figure 14. VTN Topology

Here is the VTN configuration for the controller:

```
vtn VTN1_TENANT1 {
  vbridge TENANT1_VBRIDGE1 {
    interface TO_VM_1
    interface TO_VM_2
  }
  vexternal VM_1 {
    ofs-map ofs-datapath-id 0000-0000-0000-0001 ofs-port GBE0/1 vlan-id
    10 tagged
    interface VM_1_TO_VBRIDGE
  }
  vexternal VM_2 {
    ofs-map ofs-datapath-id 0000-0000-0000-0001 ofs-port GBE0/2 vlan-id
    10 tagged
    interface VM_2_TO_VBRIDGE
```

```
    }
    vlink VBRIDGE_TO_VM_1 {
        vtn link vbridge TENANT1_VBRIDGE1 interface TO_VM_1 vtnnode VM_1 interface
VM_1_TO_VBRIDGE
    }
    vlink VBRIDGE_TO_VM_2 {
        vtn link vbridge TENANT1_VBRIDGE1 interface TO_VM_2 vtnnode VM_2 interface
VM_2_TO_VBRIDGE
    }
}
```

Once the VTN configuration is committed, the controller knows how to handle packets received from the OpenFlow switch via the OFPT_PACKET_IN message. For example, here is the ARP message from one of the VMs redirected to the controller via our flow table rule 4027 shown earlier.

```
Helpful Tip: I installed the development version of Wireshark on my Windows
laptop (v1.11.3) to decode the OpenFlow 1.0 messages properly.
```

The VTN configuration tells the controller to direct the broadcast message to port 2 of the switch as shown in the OFPT_PACKET_OUT message below.

The controller has now directed ARP frames accordingly allowing the two VMs to send unicast packets, but the first unicast packets are still redirected to the controller via OFPT_PACKET_IN messages. For VTNs, the programmable flow switch creates flows based on unicast packets received from the controller. Here is a snippet from NEC's PFC configuration guide for version 5.0 of their software:

```
The PFC, triggered by a packet reception by an OFS, determines the output
destination port according to the virtual network configuration. The flow is
determined by the input/output OFS port information and the match conditions
for the flow.

Unicast flow is dynamically created in response to the generated traffic, and
its transmission information is set in the flow table in the OFS.
```

With unicast packets being directed to the OpenFlow switch via the controller, we can now see the unicast flows installed in the switch's flow table matching on the MAC address of each VM.

```
PF5240-1# show openflow table
Date 2000/03/02 19:10:54 UTC

[OpenFlow 1]

   <pri>    <in port> <entry no><matched octets><matched packets><table>
25000 0/01 [0x00000001]   4031          212                2            exp
25000 0/02 [0x00000002]   4032          212                2            exp
23000      any            4026            0                0            nm2
 *  2 0/01 [0x00000001]   4027        18974              179            nm2
 *  2 0/02 [0x00000002]   4028          212                2            nm2
 *  2 0/03 [0x00000003]   4029            0                0            nm2
 *  2 0/04 [0x00000004]   4030            0                0            nm2

PF5240-1# show openflow table entry 4031 detail
Date 2000/03/02 19:11:22 UTC

[OpenFlow 1]

<entry 4031>
  table type               : expanded
  forwarding state         : hardware-based
  matched octets           : 3074
  matched packets          : 29
  green and yellow octets  : 3074
  green and yellow packets : 29
  red octets               : -
  red packets              : -
  idle timer(max/current)  : 300 sec / 300 sec
  hard timer(max/current)  : 0 sec / 0 sec
  priority                 : 25000
  added command            : pf flowmod
  flow flags               : SEND_PF_FLOW_REM
  added time               : 2000/03/02 19:10:50 UTC
  last modified time       : -
```

```
    flow cookie                  : 0xc800b44a000102eb

match
    match type                   : VENDOR
    input port                   : 0/01 [0x00000001]
    metadata                     : 0x0000000000000000
    src mac address              : b0c6.9a30.7640
    dst mac address              : b0c6.9a30.0bc0
    input vlan                   : 10
    input vlan pcp               : any
    ethernet type                : any

action 1
    type                         : OUTPUT
    out port                     : 0/02 [0x00000002]
```

Things are looking good now, and our VTN configuration and flow tables are allowing us to pass traffic between our two VMs.

```
NECadmin@VM-1> ping 10.10.10.62
PING 10.10.10.62 (10.10.10.62): 56 data bytes
64 bytes from 10.10.10.62: icmp_seq=0 ttl=64 time=10.955 ms
64 bytes from 10.10.10.62: icmp_seq=1 ttl=64 time=1.875 ms
64 bytes from 10.10.10.62: icmp_seq=2 ttl=64 time=1.880 ms
^C
--- 10.10.10.62 ping statistics ---
3 packets transmitted, 3 packets received, 0% packet loss
round-trip min/avg/max/stddev = 1.875/4.903/10.955/4.279 ms
```

Conclusion

Is OpenFlow real? We hope that by reading this chapter you can see that it works on a variety of platforms. The great part is that if you don't believe us you can easily try it out yourself.

Does OpenFlow solve all of your network problems? No, it does not. However, there are several places where it could make a huge difference. The following chapters describe these use cases.

5

SDN + OpenFlow Use Cases

There are many evolving use cases for Software Defined Networking that leverage, and in some cases *require*, the capabilities provided by the OpenFlow protocol. There are also many evolving SDN use cases that do not require the use of the OpenFlow protocol. This chapter will discuss the use cases that either leverage or outright require OpenFlow; and in the following chapter, we'll cover the use cases that are, for the most part, unrelated to OpenFlow.

SDN + OpenFlow Use Cases

OpenFlow is one of the primary drivers that led to the SDN revolution we are currently experiencing. However, there are other protocols that can produce a Software Defined Network and OpenFlow is only one of them. This chapter focuses on the relevant and real-life SDN use cases that leverage or require the OpenFlow protocol.

Several SDN deployment models and architectures are being discussed in many different industry forums. Many are in conflict with one another, which lends credence to the current thinking about SDN: it is still in flux and there is still no single "de facto" architecture that garners industry-wide consensus. This is one reason we are writing this book!

The Open Networking Foundation (ONF) has depicted their view of an SDN architecture.

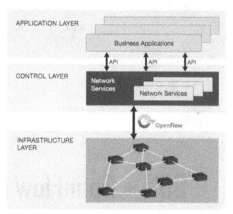

Figure 1. ONF View of SDN Architecture
[https://www.opennetworking.org/sdn-resources/sdn-definition]

This view is very OpenFlow-centric, which is logical since the ONF is the standards organization responsible for the OpenFlow specification. Other industry organizations such as the IETF are also developing their view of what an SDN architecture should look like. These other organizations include OpenFlow as one component of the overall architecture, but it is not the focal point of the architecture. In some cases, OpenFlow is not even a component in the architecture definition. For example, the FORCES WG of IETF has spent many years developing a model for the separation of the control and data planes in IP switching devices. This separation of the control and data plane is one key criteria of the SDN definition. However, OpenFlow is not part of the FORCES architecture as they have developed their own protocol and specification for the southbound API that connects the control and data plane. As another example, the Path Computation Element (PCE) WG of the IETF is also in the early stages of developing a type of SDN-based architecture for IP switching devices, primarily to support MPLS traffic engineering functions. OpenFlow is also not part of this emerging architecture definition. There are many other examples.

Before discussing details of various use cases, it is useful to categorize the use cases into one of two buckets. There are SDN solutions that focus on interacting with the data plane of network elements (e.g., a device-based programmatic model) and there are SDN solutions that focus on providing virtualized networks (e.g., an overlay-based virtualization model). These are two distinct models, yet both are considered to be SDN.

The device-based model uses one or more centralized control plane protocols, such as OpenFlow, to provide programmatic control of the network devices. This model typically modifies the forwarding state of the physical network devices. The overlay-based model uses various encapsulation (e.g., tunneling) technologies, such as VXLAN or NVGRE, to create virtualized networks. This model typically does not modify the forwarding state of the physical network devices. However, there are cases where the physical network devices are programmed to support the virtualized network; but for the most part this model provisions a logical network overlay on top of the physical network. These two models are clearly distinct, and they use different protocols and technologies.

Both of these models have corresponding use cases that are described here.

Network Virtualization

Network virtualization is not a new network requirement nor is it a new architecture. Networks have been virtualized since at least the time when Frame Relay and ATM technologies ruled the network world. Both of those are network virtualization technologies; and both are now obsolete, having been mostly replaced by MPLS. Those technologies have predominantly been deployed in wide area networks; however, ATM local area network emulation (LANE) did make a convoluted attempt to be used in local area networks. Once MPLS sufficiently replaced ATM in the WAN, it began its insertion into the LAN as well. Now MPLS VPLS technology is being used in both the LAN and the WAN. Furthermore, even traditional Ethernet LANs have been virtualized since the invention of the VLAN in the 1990s.

So, what's new with all this SDN-related network virtualization? To start with, one must remember that the recent virtualization trend started in the data center computer environment and that trend continues unabated. Most significantly, the virtualization of server resources has led to the recent boom in "cloud" data centers. This cloud-based server virtualization trend now extends into the network space, particularly the data center networking space, which has experienced very little innovation in many years. In other words, as server resources continue to be virtualized there is a requirement to virtualize the corresponding and adjacent network resources. This allows virtual machines (VM) to geographically reside anywhere in the data center, without having to manually reconfigure network devices to support the spinning up and down of new VMs and to support VM mobility.

Capabilities and functionality that correspond with network virtualization include the ability to programmatically construct and dynamically change the logical network infrastructure. Also, a key requirement is the ability to provide an agile and elastic network service. This can now be accomplished with Software Defined Networking technologies.

Data Center Virtualization

Data center virtualization is a *very* hot topic these days. Most of this activity is driven by the trend towards cloud data centers; where parts of the enterprise DC, or in some cases the entire enterprise DC, is hosted in an off-premises service provider facility. This DC cloud provider must implement a highly virtualized environment to support its many enterprise customers. The DC cloud provider must be able to provide a network service capable of large-scale multi-tenancy. The tenants of the DC cloud must operate as if they are in their own physical infrastructure, when in reality they are sharing the DC cloud providers' infrastructure with many other tenants. For enterprise DCs, multi-tenancy is also often a requirement because the enterprise may need to segment different internal business units from each other. Segmentation and multi-tenancy are often interchangeable terms when discussing data center virtualization.

So, what is the actual problem that this recent trend of network virtualization technologies solves?

Let's go back to the 1990s VLAN/802.1Q construct, which is the initial Ethernet virtualization capability. This allowed segmentation of the physical infrastructure and also allowed computers and other resources that were geographically dispersed in different physical locations inside a facility to be logically connected together at Layer 2 (i.e., in a shared broadcast domain); however, it does have scaling problems.

1. *There is only space for 4k VLANs due to the 12-bit header field for specifying the VLAN ID (VID).* While this has traditionally been a sufficient number of VLANs, in today's large-scale cloud data centers this now poses a growth and scaling limitation.

2. *While VLANs allow a logical topology to be created with less dependency on the physical infrastructure, VLANs must still be configured and mapped to network switch interfaces so that they are still inherently tied to a physical interface in the network.* The proper placement of VLANs requires advanced planning and often results in complex network configurations that are deployed into the network switches. Adds, changes, and deletes are operationally challenging. If a VLAN needs to be extended to another part of the network to accommodate a new end host connection, or more frequently these days, the move of a virtualized resource, then this requirement initiates a complex operational planning and configuration exercise. The actual implementation of those changes into the network may take hours, days, or even weeks to accomplish. This type of manual network configuration-based implementation is not only complex and labor intensive, but it also lacks efficiency and programmability.

3. *The requirement for network availability drives the need for a diverse topology.* This diverse topology equates to redundant switches and links and this topology then requires a Layer 2 network protocol to prevent loops. This typically means that a Spanning Tree Protocol (STP) is required – hardly ideal. While it does prevent loops, STP creates many problems and limitations in the network, such as slow convergence and more importantly, the need to put potentially half of the network paths into a "blocked" state in order to prevent any loops.

There are additional limitations imposed by using VLANs to provide segmentation or multi-tenancy inside a data center, but that's not the focus of this chapter.

So, a virtualized data center network is needed to meet the multi-tenancy requirement of virtualized resources. In addition, multi-tenancy and a virtualized network are needed to accommodate the mobility requirement of virtualized server resources. When VMs move to other physical machines in the DC, the logical Layer 2 topology that connects the VMs needs to move with them. Moving VLANs around to accommodate this mobility is clearly not the right answer. VMs can now be programmatically spun up and moved very rapidly and if the network needs to be manually reconfigured to accommodate the VM agility and mobility, then the network becomes the bottleneck in offering a dynamic and elastic service. The network basically "gets in the way" of providing dynamic and elastic network services. The old way of provisioning network devices no longer works in today's highly dynamic environments. The deployment rate of virtualized servers is, by far, outpacing the deployment rate of physical servers. Networks clearly need to adapt.

This is a good place to describe the virtualized logical network as an "overlay" network. Each of the virtual network topologies created equates to a logical overlay network. Underneath each of those overlay networks resides the actual physical infrastructure. The architecture of this physical infrastructure is not particularly related to the SDN discussion; however, it remains a critical part of the overall data center architecture. This physical network topology is referred to as an "underlay" network. This underlay network could run an STP but hopefully it does not. There are alternate and more efficient and productive Layer 2 network protocols and technologies available today that eliminate the need to run an STP. Transparent Interconnection of Lots of Links (TRILL) is an IETF standard protocol for providing a loop-free data center underlay network. TRILL is being developed to replace STP and RFCs 5556 and 6325 provide the TRILL specifications. TRILL uses a Layer 3 link-state routing protocol running at Layer 2 of the OSI stack to provide a loop-free environment; and without all the bad stuff that goes with the use of STP! Often this type of underlay data center network is referred to as an "Ethernet Fabric." There is even some talk about using MPLS as the data center network underlay fabric.

Another option for providing a loop-free underlay network is to use Multi-Chassis Trunking or Multi-Chassis Link Aggregation Group (LAG). However, this technology lacks industry-wide standardization and all the network vendors implement their own proprietary mechanisms. These multi-chassis technologies are vendor modifications of the standard link aggregation (IEEE 802.3ad) protocol. This modified LAG technology typically only works between two switches. In other words, it does not provide an Ethernet fabric like TRILL would; where there could be dozens of Ethernet switches operating as a single Layer 2 fabric. A common data center underlay architecture includes the access and aggregation layers of the data center being collapsed into a single Layer 2 Ethernet fabric layer; and this fabric layer is typically multi-homed to two redundant core switches using multi-chassis trunking/LAG. The Layer 3 boundary is often located at the core switches in this type of design.

Yet another option is to have a Layer 3 IP network underlay. This could be a simple OSPF network, or could even be a BGP network. The pros and cons of a Layer 2 underlay vs. a Layer 3 underlay, while extremely interesting, are outside the scope of this book.

Back to the discussion at hand – the virtualized overlay network. Interestingly, a majority of the current DC virtualization solutions do not use OpenFlow; in some cases, they may use OpenFlow as part of the overall solution but OpenFlow does not provide the overlay functionality. In these solutions, some form of encapsulation technology provides the overlay functionality. OpenFlow is not an encapsulation technology.

Technologies such as Virtual eXtensible LAN (VXLAN) or Network Virtualization using Generic Routing Encapsulation (NVGRE), and possibly even MPLS, are needed to provide the actual overlay network. Endpoints are encapsulated by one of these technologies and the interconnection of these encapsulated endpoints creates the virtualized overlay network. MPLS is mentioned as part of this discussion because MPLS has provided this type of logical network overlay in the WAN for over a decade. In a WAN environment, the MPLS encapsulated endpoints reside in PE routers instead of in data center vSwitches or pSwitches. Recent activity within the IETF has indicated a possible desire to leverage well-known WAN MPLS protocols in the data center to provide this type of intra-DC overlay network. WAN protocols such as MPLS could possibly be used for inter-DC connectivity as well. More on that specific topic later, as the virtualized network use case that does not rely on OpenFlow will be discussed in the next chapter.

Nicira, now part of VMware, provides an example of leveraging the OpenFlow protocol as part of an overall intra-DC overlay solution. This solution relies on encapsulation to provide the multi-tenancy overlay network but also relies on the OpenFlow protocol to program the required forwarding state at the tunnel endpoints. This overlay network provides Layer 2 connectivity, over the underlay network, which could be Layer 2 or Layer 3. Network forwarding state at the edge of the network is needed to map VM MAC addresses into the appropriate encapsulated "tunnel". This solution builds L2 tunnels using its NSX platform and relies on Open vSwitch (OVS) to implement the hypervisor-to-hypervisor soft switching capability.

Another example of a solution for providing an intra-DC virtual overlay network is offered by Contrail, now part of Juniper. This solution does not rely on the OpenFlow protocol for programming forwarding state, as it leverages the BGP protocol in the control plane. XMPP is used to provision the necessary state in the server hypervisor. This is one example where traditional WAN technologies, such as MPLS and BGP, are being leveraged in the data center solution space.

One example where OpenFlow could be leveraged to provide some form of isolation or segmentation capability, instead of using encapsulation, is using OpenFlow rules to force traffic from particular sources to be forwarded over particular ports or VLANs. These OpenFlow rules would forward traffic in such a manner that it provides a form of segmentation that is needed for multi-tenancy. Multi-tenancy is not the use case that OpenFlow was intended to solve. However, the use of Access Control Lists (ACL) combined with Policy Based Routing (PBR) has historically provided similar functionality in corner case deployments. ACLs + PBR functionality was not intended to provide this type of segmentation capability either, but it has been used in unique circumstances. This is a "brute-force" solution for providing some form of multi-tenancy and is not elegant, to say the least. This type of solution may pose compliance challenges as well, as the traffic from one tenant could be intermixed with traffic from another tenant due to an erroneous PBR rule. These same concerns would hold true if using OpenFlow to provide this type of segmentation. In addition, this type of solution would likely pose scalability challenges regarding the number of OpenFlow rules needed to be supported in each of the networking devices, as well as the operational challenge of managing all those OpenFlow rules. So, one could use the OpenFlow protocol to instantiate entries in networking devices such that only specific end hosts can forward traffic to other specific end hosts. This would have to be done hop-by-hop and all the OpenFlow rules would need to be consistent across the data center switching infrastructure. While this would be possible, it is clearly not optimal.

Having said that, it's fair to say that this type of solution for providing multi-tenancy should be considered the exception rather than the norm.

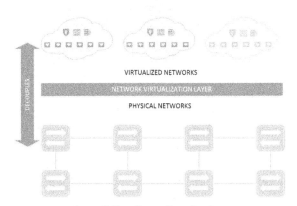

Figure 2. Data Center Virtualization

WAN Virtualization

The WAN use case for providing virtualization using OpenFlow is somewhat similar to the previous DC use case discussion; where the OpenFlow protocol could be used to provide this capability but is currently not the preferred technology. OpenFlow rules can provide a form of segmentation, also similar to which could be accomplished with ACLs + PBR rules. While scale is a concern, using OpenFlow is more desirable than using ACLs + PBR. ACLs + PBR configurations in networking devices will quickly become complex and unwieldy, and they are very subject to human error. Using OpenFlow for this type of segmentation is operationally easier to deploy and manage, as all the complexity is hidden in the SDN layer and is not prone to human CLI configuration error. In addition, the configuration of the networking devices is much simpler when using OpenFlow for this type of solution rather than using ACLs + PBR rules. Imagine a router configuration loaded with 100-plus ACL + PBR rules, or even 1000-plus rules!

While using OpenFlow to replace complex and error-prone ACL + PBR configurations is possible in the WAN, OpenFlow is rather used to "nail-up" Layer 2 virtual connections in the WAN. These Layer 2 virtual connections result in a virtualized WAN topology. For example, assume a Layer 2 service where two customers are connected across a WAN over a common VLAN. Further assume that this VLAN spans many networking devices (i.e., routers and switches) in the WAN. Standard VLAN configurations in network switches or routers could create this service; however, the configurations are manually implemented and the VLAN-IDs along the path and at the endpoints usually must match. Each network device is manually configured with VLAN IDs that correspond to this single Point-to-Point (P2P) Layer 2 service. While VLAN translation is possible, it results in additional operational complexity. Alternately, an MPLS pseudo-wire could be provisioned to connect the two customer VLAN segments into a single P2P service. This can also be a somewhat complex exercise, requiring pre-planning and often complex configurations in the PE nodes. Additionally, an MPLS signaling protocol must be run in the WAN. Having said that, this type of P2P Layer 2 service using MPLS is currently very common in service provider networks. Could an SDN-based OpenFlow solution provide a similar service in a simpler and more programmatic manner?

Internet2 offers an Advanced Layer 2 Service (AL2S) using OpenFlow rules in networking devices to provide a P2P Layer 2 service across its national backbone network. This service is part of their Internet2 Innovation Platform offering; and this network is managed by the GlobalNOC at Indiana University. This is a deployed Software Defined Networking service that directly leverages the capabilities provided by OpenFlow. While this service can now be characterized as a WAN virtualization service, it started as a dynamic Layer 2 provisioning service rather than a virtualization service. You can find more information about this service at the URL below.

http://noc.net.internet2.edu/i2network/advanced-layer-2-service.html

Customers of Internet2 can provision point-to-point VLANs to other Internet2 customers using the AL2S web portal. The motivation for this service is the requirement to quickly provision new virtual networks (here's that *network agility* buzzword again). The software allows customers of Internet2 to request and rapidly provision Layer 2 virtual networks. This eliminates the long provisioning delays that are often associated with creating these types of Layer 2 virtual networks over the WAN.

In AL2S, the Open Science, Scholarship & Services Exchange (OS3E) software that customers use talks to an OpenFlow controller to push OpenFlow rules into the many Internet2 networking devices (that happen to be 100 GbE switches). This software-based provisioning system basically "nails-up" a VLAN between customers across the network backbone in a very dynamic manner. Sounds like SDN, doesn't it? Furthermore, multi-tenancy is a key component of this service. The initial design was to offer this SDN service on top of the existing IP production network, as it would be cost prohibitive to build a new network to offer this innovative SDN service. Currently, the I2 IP network operates on top of the OF provisioned L2 network. Multiple customers can provision their own virtual Layer 2 networks, in essence, sharing the physical infrastructure. So, the WAN is indeed virtualized.

In this type of service, the VLAN IDs do not need to match on each end of the P2P connection since OpenFlow rules can perform any necessary VLAN translation on any of the networking nodes in the path. This eliminates the burden of matching VLAN IDs on each end of the L2 service, which, previously, often became a bottleneck in terms of coordination and provisioning. Now there is no need for coordination of specific VLAN IDs between two different customers that are connected over the A2LS service.

A critical component of this service is the need for some form of *hybrid* OpenFlow switch. As previously discussed, most OpenFlow switches come in two categories: 1) the entire switch is only capable of OpenFlow and, 2) some ports on the switch are under the control of OpenFlow while other ports on the switch are configured by traditional means. If this type of service were offered using the category 1 type of OpenFlow switches, then it would be necessary to build an entirely new network for this service — an infeasible and cost-prohibitive option. If this service is provided by the category 2 type of switches, these switches could also provide traditional L2/L3 service; however, the OpenFlow network would still operate as a parallel physical infrastructure. New circuits would be needed to provide the AL2S service to connect the OpenFlow-only switch interfaces, so this network would run in parallel to the existing L2/L3 network.

What is needed is another level of granularity in the hybrid switch. Not only should some ports be dedicated to OpenFlow while others are dedicated to traditional L2/L3 protocols, some ports should be able to run _both_ OpenFlow and traditional L2/L3 protocols simultaneously. This is a true hybrid OpenFlow switch. Internet2 could offer the AL2S service on the existing L2/L3 infrastructure with no need to build a parallel network. What they ultimately deployed is more of a pure OF provisioned backbone that also provides the IP services. Said another way, the OpenFlow network runs as a virtualized topology along with the existing L2/L3 production network and this service is provisioned using SDN. This can be described as network virtualization or network slicing. This network has been deployed for almost three years now.

While this is one real-life example of an SDN-based WAN, other examples are being developed as the technology continues to evolve. One question that has already been asked in various industry forums is whether OpenFlow could replace existing deployed technologies, such as MPLS, in providing a virtualized WAN service. Some ponder this question "tongue-in-cheek" while others are trying to determine if this might actually be feasible one day soon. We will discuss this possibility of a "hybrid SDN" in another chapter.

Network Service Chaining, Dynamic Service Insertion, Service Function Chaining, and Traffic Steering

While the title of this particular section includes four different topics, they are basically the same use case being described by four different descriptions. This is a very important and relevant use case and many of the largest global service providers have been publicly discussing aspects of this use case in various industry forums and events. Some providers are in the early stages of deploying this type of service and others are testing various aspects of this use case in their labs. Solving this use case with traditional mechanisms has been problematic for many years in service provider networks; so this has been a problem waiting for a viable solution. Now that OpenFlow is available, it appears to be one of the right technologies to solve the problem.

The Problem Statement

The problem is a fairly basic one but it has challenged service providers for many years. Service providers need to optimize their network infrastructure to allow services to be inserted dynamically and efficiently. Their revenue models also require new service offerings. Today, service insertion is not performed in a way that can be even remotely called "efficient." The "traffic steering" description relates more to the solution than to the "service insertion" problem. Traffic needs to be steered in such a way to allow for the dynamic and efficient service insertion capability. Examples of services that need to be inserted into the traffic path include DPI, firewall, load balancing, and others.

The IETF is also working to define this problem and to provide an industry standardized solution to the problem. Initially, the IETF formed a Network Service Chaining (NSC) Birds of a Feather (BOF) to openly discuss the various aspects of this use case. The ensuing activity soon led to the formal creation of a Service Function Chaining (SFC) WG. Please see:

---

http://datatracker.ietf.org/doc/draft-ietf-sfc-problem-statement/

As described in the problem statement, service insertion refers to the deployment of a service whereby the service provider needs to specify an ordered list of services (i.e., service chaining) that should be applied to an individual traffic flow. A critical component of this use case is a capability to "steer traffic" through the ordered list of services. This problem space is quickly becoming tightly coupled with the Network Function Virtualization (NFV) work being done at the European Telecommunications Standards Institute (ETSI) and the IETF. The NFV work at ETSI and IETF is fairly new activity, most of it having been initiated in 2013. At IETF 87 in Berlin, Germany in the summer of 2013, the first BOF meeting was held to initiate open discussion on Network Service Chaining (NSC). While the NSC BOF did not ultimately result in a formal IETF NSC WG, a Service Function Chaining (SFC) WG has now been formed to address this problem space.

---

http://datatracker.ietf.org/wg/sfc/charter/

Today, service is inserted into the traffic path in an inefficient and cumbersome manner. In addition, the service delivery mechanisms are rapidly experiencing significant change due to the rise of virtualization technologies that we have discussed in this book. Some service providers have a traffic steering "application" that might be centralized in a data center. User traffic is funneled to this traffic steering application and services are then provided. This leads to inefficient use of network resources and often results in "tromboning" of user traffic across the provider's network. Services are often topology-dependent; meaning, they are located at specific points in the network. Traditional IP routing cannot provide a level of granularity that is required for proper service insertion. The service insertion is often required at the "IP flow" level of granularity. IP routing is purely "IP destination" based and does not provide the required IP flow level of granularity. To make matters more difficult, services are moving toward a topology-independent architecture. Virtualization and network overlays are driving this requirement to insert services in a topology-independent manner.

As one simple example of the need for a granular traffic steering capability, imagine a need to steer user email traffic to a security appliance but the provider does not want all traffic to that user to be steered through the security appliance (e.g., video traffic). IP routing cannot distinguish between different types of traffic going to the same destination. Complex Access-Control List (ACL) and Policy-Based Routing (PBR) configurations could be used to direct traffic at the required IP flow level, but ACL + PBR configurations are a complex and cumbersome answer to this problem. It's an answer, but it's the wrong answer. In addition, these types of configurations are very vendor-specific and are typically configured manually by a network administrator or operator. The routers' configuration file will become quite large and unwieldy when many of these ACL + PBR configurations are in place to steer traffic around the network. To add to the current difficulties in providing this type of service with existing protocols, the current mechanisms are not capable of being agile enough in terms of programmability. They are reactive, manually implemented configurations that often take days or weeks to implement into the network. These configuration and policy enforcement tasks require significant effort due to the lack of a common control protocol or interface to the various network devices.

Enter stage left – OpenFlow!

As mentioned previously, OpenFlow appears to be the right technology at the right time to solve the problem of network service function chaining. A simple OpenFlow rule produces the same result as a complex ACL + PBR configuration. And OpenFlow rules are pushed into the network from a logically centralized controller that houses intelligent software. This combination of components and protocols creates a Software Defined Network; and it is this SDN layer that implements the required network service function chaining capability.

A network switch or router can be programmed by OpenFlow to implement rules needed to steer traffic flows on a node-by-node basis, providing the requisite service chaining capability. These rules can be pushed into physical hardware devices, like network switches and routers, or into virtualized network devices that might run on multi-core x86 computer resources. The end result is the same— a specific traffic flow is steered to the appropriate network devices (physical or virtual) to properly insert the service. This can be accomplished via OpenFlow at the IP destination layer of granularity, or at the IP flow layer of granularity. This service chaining capability allows the service provider to insert services at the appropriate place in the network, in a very programmatic and efficient manner.

The network device configurations are also greatly simplified, as no ACL + PBR policies are required. The state of all the service chaining rules is maintained in the intelligent software that runs on top of the controller. Telstra, Verizon, and NTT are a few of many large service providers that have publicly described their requirements and plans for service chaining using OpenFlow. Some of these carriers have publicly said that they are conducting field trials with plans to operationalize this capability in their production network in the 2014-2015 timeframe.

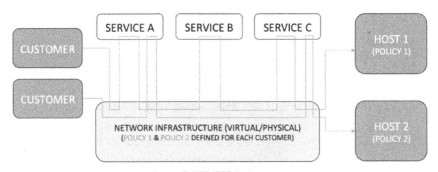

Figure 3. NSC/SFC Architecture

A related capability for pushing ACL-like rules into network devices is an available and industry standardized mechanism, RFC 5575, Dissemination of Flow Specifications Rules. This leverages the highly interoperable and deployed BGP control plane to instantiate these traffic flow rules, or ACLs, into the network devices. The primary use case for BGP flowspec is for Distributed Denial of Service (DDoS) mitigation and not service chaining; however, the capability appears similar at a high level. One critical difference is that this is a distributed control plane solution that requires the devices to run BGP; whereas the service chaining solution that leverages OpenFlow is a logically centralized SDN solution. Is it fair to say it's kind of like "old school" vs. "new school"?

Any relevant discussion of NSC/SFC requires that Network Function Virtualization (NFV) be mentioned. NFV is a requirement that has existed for many years from all top Tier-1 service providers, but really came to the forefront with SDN in late 2012 and has been a very visible SDN topic in 2013. The world's top carriers have recently publicized a second version of their white paper on the need for NFV, titled: "Network Function Virtualization: An Introduction, Benefits, Enablers, Challenges and Call for Action." It is authored by many of the largest global network operators. The following text from the Executive Summary summarizes this much needed SDN-enabled capability very well.

> Network Operators' networks are populated with a large and increasing variety of proprietary hardware appliances. To launch a new network service often requires yet another variety and finding the space and power to accommodate these boxes is becoming increasingly difficult; compounded by the increasing costs of energy, capital investment challenges and the rarity of skills necessary to design, integrate and operate increasingly complex hardware-based

appliances. Moreover, hardware-based appliances rapidly reach end of life, requiring much of the procure-design-integrate-deploy cycle to be repeated with little or no revenue benefit. Worse, hardware lifecycles are becoming shorter as technology and services innovation accelerates, inhibiting the roll out of new revenue earning network services and constraining innovation in an increasingly network-centric connected world.

Network Functions Virtualisation aims to address these problems by leveraging standard IT virtualisation technology to consolidate many network equipment types onto industry standard high volume servers, switches and storage, which could be located in Datacentres, Network Nodes and in the end user premises. We believe Network Functions Virtualisation is applicable to any data plane packet processing and control plane function in fixed and mobile network infrastructures.

NFV will be covered in detail in Chapter 6, so we will not discuss it further here.

Note that while SDN enables such a capability, a full software-defined network is not absolutely required to provide NFV. The NFV and SDN technologies are clearly aligned and mutually beneficial to each other, but they are not so bound to each other that they cannot function independently.

Recent activity within the IETF and ETSI is looking at implementing the service function chain as yet another overlay. This would be an elegant solution, even compared to an OF-based one. However, this is very early work and no clear encapsulations are yet defined. This work is being described here.

[https://datatracker.ietf.org/doc/draft-quinn-sfc-nsh/]

Network Monitoring and Analytics

Network monitoring and analytics are gaining wider acceptance from network operators, in both the service provider and enterprise communities. The need to glean information *from* the network in an automated fashion is key part of the SDN story that is often overlooked. Most people think of SDN in terms of provisioning and programming state *into* the network. SDN must be a full-duplex architecture; it's not just about programming state into the network. Extracting state and analytics information from the network is increasingly important to manage the network in the most cost-effective and efficient manner.

There are many reasons for needing detailed and real-time network analytics. There are security use cases, lawful intercept use cases, network performance monitoring and tuning use cases, and many others. There are two basic types of analytics that can be gleaned from networks: one from the inline/in-band network devices (production switches and routers) and another from out-of-band network devices.

Examples of inline/in-band network analytic capabilities are sFlow and NetFlow. Network devices can capture and send sFlow information to an sFlow collector and the network operator can glean valuable information about the network from the powerful graphing and analytic capabilities of various sFlow collectors. InMon is a leading vendor for sFlow. There is an sFlow-RT (Real Time) capability being developed; where the collector receives sFlow information and can analyze the samples in near real-time. Based on that result, an SDN application can program state into the network using OpenFlow. This could be useful for traffic engineering purposes, for example. The example below from InMon shows how sFlow and OpenFlow can work together to provide a comprehensive SDN solution.

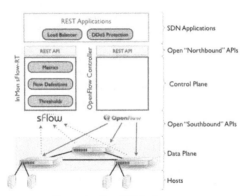

Figure 4. sFlow SDN Architecture
[http://blog.sflow.com/2013/03/ddos.html]

While this example shows a load balancing and DDoS prevention application, many other applications in the SDN layer of this solution could leverage the network data that sFlow can provide.

OpenFlow can also aid in the exporting of traffic for analytics purposes. OpenFlow rules in network switches and routers can copy data packet flows as they traverse through the device, sending these duplicated packet flows out different interfaces where analytics devices are connected.

The out-of-band network analytic capability also presents an interesting use case for OpenFlow. A passive, out-of-band network analytics capability is deployed in telecom service providers. This type of capability has been deployed for many years;

however, the provisioning of this type of solution is cumbersome, not really automated, and not sufficiently dynamic in terms of real-time updates. Basically, network switches are placed out-of-band alongside the production network devices. Traffic is tapped or spanned to these passive network switches. How that happens is not important to this use case. What is important is that the analytic switches receive the production traffic in a non-disruptive and passive manner.

Now comes the interesting part. These switches are then configured with ACLs and PBR rules to allow them to split out *interesting* traffic flows and send those flows out a specific port or groups of ports. Network analytic devices are connected to these ports; and it's these devices that perform the actual analytics function. The network switch is merely filtering traffic, based on an ACL matching rule, and is sending that traffic out a specific port or set of ports, based on PBR rules. There is intelligent analytic software in the Application Layer that turns the captured data into meaningful graphs and charts for the network operator. The operator can then re-provision the analytics switch when different types of traffic flows need to be analyzed. This re-provisioning could be automated by software but is often a manual process. Usually there are scripts written to push new ACL + PBR configurations into the analytics switches, rather than having an operator on the Command Line Interface (CLI), but in either case it's not really automated and the resulting configuration on the analytics switch is complex and quite large. All of this makes this solution operationally difficult to deploy and manage.

Here is where OpenFlow can greatly simplify the operation of this solution. Remember that OpenFlow basically mimics the behavior of an ACL by matching on a specific traffic flow and it mimics the behavior of a PBR rule by sending that traffic out a specific interface. This is exactly what is required on the analytics switch. The network operator can now use intelligent software that pushes OpenFlow rules into the switches, rather than pushing ACL + PBR configurations into the switch. This is a perfect use case for SDN + OpenFlow. This now becomes a fully automated and dynamic network analytics solution that perfectly leverages the capabilities of SDN + OpenFlow.

A real example of this capability is available from Big Switch Networks. Their Big Tap monitoring application orchestrates an OpenFlow fabric to filter and deliver traffic from any TAP/SPAN port to any analytics tool. The diagram below shows how this application works. The Big Switch OpenFlow controller runs the Big Tap monitoring software and this controller pushes the OpenFlow rules into the OpenFlow-enabled switched infrastructure. Network traffic is split in the production network into this passive monitoring fabric. The OpenFlow rules then filter on specific traffic flows and directs those flows to the appropriate analytics device.

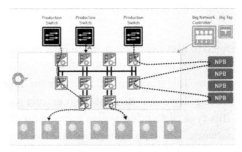

Figure 5. Big Switch Big Tap SDN Application
[http://www.bigswitch.com/products/big-tap-network-monitoring]

Brocade also demonstrated a similar network monitoring and analytics capability at the Open Networking Summit (ONS) in 2013. The solution is depicted here.

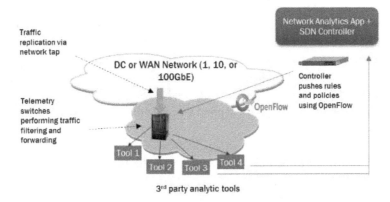

Figure 6. Brocade's Network Analytics SDN Demo
[http://community.brocade.com/t5/Attend-Events/Brocade-SDN-Analytics-Application-Demo/ta-p/1285]

This demonstration leverages the OpenFlow protocol for installing the policy rules into the monitoring device instead of using legacy mechanisms such as ACLs and PBR. The analytics application is the intelligent software that provides the analysis capability and also determines, with operator input, which types of traffic is forwarding to the various analytics devices. Similar to the Big Switch solution, the production network is tapped and traffic is non-disruptively and passively forwarded to the analytics switches.

As you can see, these are basically the same solution for leveraging the powerful capabilities of OpenFlow to create an SDN solution for network monitoring and analytics.

IETF I2RS

While not directly related to network analytics, the Interface to the Routing System (I2RS) WG of the IETF is working towards providing a standardized interface into the network routing system. This standardized interface (or interfaces) will not only program state into routing devices, but it will also extract state from these same routing devices. So, this type of solution is also focused on gleaning analytics information from the network. This is an example of an SDN strategy, as it intends to leverage an intelligent software layer; however, it may not be similar to the logically centralized view of a traditional SDN architecture. The I2RS architecture is more similar to the hybrid network concept previously discussed. In the I2RS architecture, traditional distributed protocols such as OSPF, ISIS, and BGP continue to operate in the network, but an intelligent software layer exists outside of this distributed networking layer. This intelligent software layer can provide additional networking capabilities by rapidly reacting to networking events and modifying the routing parameters of the network. This potentially centralized software works in conjunction with the distributed networking protocols, not as a replacement to them. The I2RS interface communicates with the control plane Routing Information Base (RIB) of the networking devices, not the data plane Forwarding Information Base (FIB). This is different from the OpenFlow-enabled SDN architecture; where in this architecture the OpenFlow protocol programs state directly into the data plane FIB of networking devices.

The I2RS continues to be ongoing work area in the IETF, as this WG was only formed in late 2012 and the charter is being re-defined. Additional details of I2RS are discussed in Chapter 6.

Traffic Engineering

Traffic engineering is another very real use case for SDN and OpenFlow. In fact, this is a currently deployed solution in Google's production Inter-DC network. They refer to this internal network as their "G-scale" backbone, while their Internet-facing network is the "I-scale" backbone. The G-scale network provides Inter-DC connectivity only; it does not provide Internet-facing or Intra-DC connectivity. Having said that, Intra-DC traffic engineering will be a relevant SDN use case in the near future. There are already requirements and solutions for Intra-DC traffic engineering deployed today but migrating these solutions to SDN has yet to gain much traction in the DC space. On this topic, BGP is deployed inside the DC to meet Intra-DC traffic engineering and scaling requirements. BGP is typically used purely as a WAN protocol. So, Intra-DC traffic engineering is a real requirement in the large scale cloud data centers, but the topic of this specific use case is all about Inter-DC connectivity.

When discussing the need for service provider WAN traffic engineering, MPLS is usually the first technology that comes to mind. MPLS traffic engineering is a widely deployed solution in practically every global service provider's network. The need to efficiently use the expensive infrastructure becomes paramount not only in cost savings but also in providing strict SLAs to customers. Circuit upgrades are a time consuming and costly process, so if the network operator can delay an expensive circuit upgrade by moving traffic to an underutilized portion of their network, then the cost savings are obvious and immediately realized. Simply put, MPLS-based traffic engineering allows the network operator to forward traffic over the non-shortest paths in the network. IGPs, such as OSPF and ISIS, build a loop-free topology based on a shortest path graph that each node calculates. All traffic to a particular destination follows the same shortest path in the network. RSVP-TE provides enhanced traffic engineering capabilities, in addition to providing other features such as Fast Re-Route (FRR).

IGP link metric tuning is also a valid and deployed traffic engineering solution in both enterprise and service provider networks. However, this does not provide the granularity required in service provider networks. IGP-based TE leverages a distributed routing protocol to discover the network topology, react to changes in the topology, and runs an algorithm to determine the shortest-path to other endpoints in the topology. MPLS offers an additional benefit of providing traffic engineering over the non-shortest path, which not only provides an enhanced granularity to distribute traffic loads over different network paths but also provides the ability to differentiate traffic types for CoS/QoS purposes.

A modified shortest path algorithm is run in MPLS/RSVP-TE networks, called Constrained Shortest Path First (CSPF). CSPF provides the ability for the LSP to take any available path in the network and it is no longer restricted to the shortest path calculated by the IGP. The operator can traffic engineer an LSP to take a less than optimal path across its network, from a link metric or delay perspective, to avoid highly used "hot spots" in the network. This delays or prevents the need to upgrade the link that is experiencing congestion, since traffic is moved to other available and under-utilized links in the network.

This use case warrants a higher-level discussion of whether OpenFlow can solve traffic engineering requirements that can't already be solved with existing protocols. Since MPLS already provides a very robust traffic engineering capability, why bother trying to use SDN + OpenFlow instead? At an abstract level one can question the trade-offs between distributed and centralized control planes. The MPLS control plane is clearly distributed; it needs a distributed IGP (OSPF or ISIS) and it also needs a distributed label allocation protocol (LDP or RSVP). The SDN + OpenFlow traffic engineering use case relies on a centralized control plane. This centralized control plane actually needs to be somewhat distributed for redundancy reasons, so this is called a "logically centralized" control plane. It makes no sense to have a single centralized SDN controller in a network since that presents a glaring single point of failure. The network requires at least two SDN controllers, and these controllers must maintain state between them to remain synchronized and support some form of high availability. Initially this is expected to be an "active/passive" configuration but eventually it could evolve into an "all active" configuration. This high-availability requirement presents a complex problem currently being examined and addressed by the ONF, the IETF, and other organizations such as the OpenDaylight project.

The SDN + OpenFlow use case relies on centralized software sitting on top of OpenFlow controllers, emulating and controlling the production network topology and forwarding state. It requires analytics data from the network—including link utilization, congestion, and possibly even router queuing statistics in real time—to properly model the topology. Some of this data can be gathered from the network using protocols such as sFlow, or by using other standard or proprietary mechanisms. Once the software properly emulates and models the network topology and resources, traffic engineering decisions can be made and implemented into the network. The goal is to provide optimal network performance for all network users as efficiently as possible. A properly traffic-engineered network can provide strict SLA guarantees and delay the need to upgrade circuits, since traffic loads can be distributed optimally across the network. OpenFlow could be the protocol of choice to implement traffic engineering rules into the network on a *per-flow* basis. This granular traffic engineering capability is difficult for MPLS-based mechanisms to provide. Often the MPLS-based solutions for these granular TE decisions are difficult to implement and operationally complex to manage.

So, there two basic questions: 1) Does SDN/OpenFlow-TE offer capabilities not available with MPLS/RSVP-TE? 2) If SDN/OpenFlow-TE provides the same capability as MPLS/RSVP-TE, is it much simpler to engineer, deploy, and operate?

Let's tackle these questions one at a time. First, there is no denying that MPLS/RSVP-TE is a widely deployed technology that is continually being enhanced to provide dynamic and scalable traffic engineering functionality. The FRR and Auto-Bandwidth (Auto-BW) features are two prime examples of the continued innovation in this technology. While it is the de-facto WAN traffic engineering solution, it has some generally accepted restrictions.

MPLS/RSVP-TE Challenges

Right off the top, there is a restriction in MPLS-based solutions regarding the "flooding scope" of IGP traffic engineering information. Due to the restriction in OSPF and ISIS that LSAs/LSPs that include traffic engineering information can be limited in flooding scope to a single OSPF area or ISIS level, inter-area or inter-level traffic engineering is by default not possible. While extensions are now available to overcome this limitation, they are complex, not supported by all vendors, and not widely deployed in production networks. In addition, inter-domain MPLS traffic engineering is even more complex and even less deployed.

A common argument against MPLS/RSVP-TE is that it is too operationally complex to deploy and manage. In addition to the multiple protocols required in the network, the operational challenges of MPLS router configurations and more specifically, the challenges associated with the optimization of RSVP LSPs, can become very difficult to properly manage. Often a staff of MPLS experts is required to fully design, test, deploy, and manage an MPLS/RSVP-TE solution. Also, operators may face vendor interoperability limitations that are discovered only when their production network experiences an outage.

The lack of native IPv6 forwarding support in LDP and RSVP-TE is gaining wider attention. At the Orlando IETF 86 in early 2013, this was a topic of discussion in the MPLS WG. Operators expressed that it is time to finally support native IPv6 signaling in the LDP and RSVP-TE protocols. There are Internet Drafts for native IPv6 MPLS signaling, but software development for this has not been a priority in vendor roadmaps. And, it will be years before vendor gear is implemented for this in an interoperable manner. One reason for this slow progress is that most service providers run an IPv4-only core and run an IPv4/IPv6 dual-stack capability only at the edge of the network. IPv6 edge traffic is tunneled in MPLS through the IPv4 core. So, providers offer IPv6 services today without having to actually implement IPv6 or a dual-stack in their core network. Due to this architecture, the lack of native IPv6 signaling in MPLS may not pose a significant current concern but it's worth noting.

MPLS/RSVP-TE is inherently a distributed solution. Each node runs its respective protocols with its adjacent neighbors and each node builds its own Traffic Engineering Database (TED), just like each node builds its own Link-State Database (LSDB). While the distributed nature of these protocols has allowed the solution to function at Internet-scale, each node computes all the traffic engineering decisions locally. There is no real-time global view of the entire system from a traffic engineering perspective. The lack of a global view can cause engineering and operational problems in the network, including a lack of predictability and deterministic scheduling of LSPs. If many LSPs are signaled in roughly the same time interval, the actual order of the LSP setup may become unpredictable, depending on vendor implementation. Also, it may be desired and optimal to schedule the setup of LSPs in a specific order to fully optimize the network—this capability is not possible with the current MPLS/RSVP-TE distributed solution.

The lack of global view can also cause bin-packing problems, or the inability to dynamically re-shuffle LSPs over different links when the actual traffic demand exceeds the capacity of a particular link. Although features such as automatic bandwidth (Auto-BW) are now available to mitigate these issues, this further complicates the network. And the Auto-BW decisions are still run independently by each router; so while a single router may be able to re-shuffle its LSPs based on its own bandwidth demands, the router lacks a global view of the network bandwidth demands and its actions may result in congestion for LSPs originating from other routers. This does not provide global optimization.

While software tools are available that provide a global view of a traffic engineered network, these tools are often expensive and they require a high level of expertise to fully utilize. These tools are not typically used for real-time decisions; they are typically used in an "off-line" method. Furthermore, these tools do not solve all the problems associated with running a distributed traffic engineering solution.

Another problem is an LSP deadlock condition where the bandwidth demand of one LSP increases but the other LSPs sharing a link with that LSP are unaware of the demand increase, resulting in the combined actual traffic load exceeding the link capacity. This is due to the lack of a standardized admission control mechanism at the LSP ingress node. The manifestation of this condition exists when the RSVP-TE control plane and associated data in the TED is out of sync with the actual data plane link capacities. Auto-BW also attempts to mitigate this condition but as already explained, it is not a widely deployed feature and it remains a distributed feature that is run independently on each node. The local node's decision to modify its bandwidth can also distort any real-time global view of the network resources.

CPU and memory constraints on the MPLS router nodes may become an area of concern. Since each node runs multiple control plane protocols (OSPF/ISIS, LDP/RSVP-TE, and BGP) and maintains multiple databases (TED and LSDB), there may be cases where the router control plane becomes overloaded. This can cause instability in the network. This is further exacerbated by the fact that router control plane CPU and memory upgrades are dictated by router vendor product roadmaps. If this control plane is de-coupled and resides outside the router chassis, for example in a multi-core x86 computing device, the network provider could upgrade the performance of the control plane hardware without having any dependency on the router vendor.

The RSVP-TE soft-state that is required in all the LSRs in the network often imposes a control plane scalability concern. The desired architecture for an RSVP-TE network is a full mesh of LSPs. But this raises a scale problem and mechanisms have been added to MPLS to scale this type of network; such as Hierarchical RSVP and LDP-over-RSVP. This adds additional complexity. A new IETF WG has been chartered, called the Source Packet Routing in Networking (SPRING) WG, to address some of this scale concern. This type of architecture requires some sort of offline intelligence; somewhat resembling an SDN-like architecture.

SDN/OpenFlow-TE Comparison

One clear distinction between MPLS/RSVP-TE and SDN/OpenFlow-TE is the logi-cally centralized control plane and the clear separation of the networking hardware in the data plane from the networking software in the control plane. This logically centralized control plane is expected to have a global view of the networking in-frastructure's resource usage. With a global view it is expected that the SDN traffic engineering application can optimize the topology in a more deterministic, predict-able, and efficient manner. Some of the identified issues with RSVP-TE, such as the bin-packing problem and some deadlock conditions, might be avoided. Well, that's the current thinking anyway.

Running the traffic engineering solution as a logically centralized software applica-tion also allows for feature innovation velocity, where new features can be rapidly implemented in software. Once tested and validated, the resulting actions can be pushed into the network data plane. This eliminates the need to upgrade the fea-ture set of each router in the network in order to take advantage of a new feature. Additionally, accurately emulating the network topology in software creates a test lab environment where new features can be tested and iterative "what-if" traffic-en-gineering decisions can be simulated without pushing new actions into the network data plane—a very powerful capability. While the previously mentioned MPLS/RSVP-TE traffic engineering tools provide a simulated "what-if" capability, they are not fully integrated solutions. They do not receive network resource state and events in real-time, nor do they push new traffic engineering rules or actions back into the network in real-time. They are used offline and typically any updates or changes recommended by these tools are scheduled during a network maintenance window.

Holistic Global View

A holistic global view of network resource usage also eliminates any restrictions on IGP area/level flooding scope. The centralized traffic engineering application has a global view of the network and is not restricted to only receiving information about a single IGP area or level. So, the inter-area or inter-level restriction in an MPLS solution is being addressed with an SDN solution. However, the inter-domain traffic engineering complexity that was previously discussed remains a complex problem to solve, even with SDN/OpenFlow-TE. To provide an inter-domain traffic engineering capability, each of the logically centralized applications would need to exchange net-work state with the other applications that exist in neighboring domains. This is not a trivial problem to solve. The bottom line is that the problem of inter-domain traffic engineering remains a complex issue that needs further innovation for both MPLS/RSVP-TE and SDN/OpenFlow-TE solutions. This type of capability also makes high availability a more complex problem to solve.

Among other organizations, the OpenDaylight foundation, formed in 2013, is examining the problem of highly available, yet centralized, control plane architectures. They refer to this capability as a "cluster of controller nodes," leveraging the OpenDaylight SDN Controller Platform (OSCP). From their public website:

While OSCP is logically centralized, the controller is installed on multiple controller-nodes for redundancy and scale. Each controller-node is simply a separate installed image of the software (or separate hardware appliances with the software installed on it). All the controller-nodes communicate with each other to form a controller cluster, where each node in the cluster shares information with other nodes in the cluster to ensure availability in case any node fails.

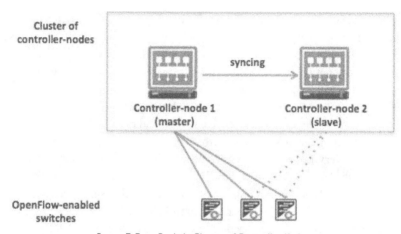

Figure 7. Open Daylight Cluster of Controller Nodes

[https://wiki.opendaylight.org/view/OpenDaylight_SDN_Controller_Platform_ (OSCP):Main#The_Three-Tier_Architecture:_OpenDaylight_Virtualization_ Platform.2C_Switches.2C_and_Applications]

The operational complexity differences with an SDN/OpenFlow-TE solution are yet to be proven one way or another. There isn't sufficient real-world experience to determine if a logically centralized traffic engineering solution is indeed easier to implement and manage as compared to a distributed MPLS-based solution. One certainty is that there exists quite a bit of expert level MPLS engineering and operational experience in today's networking community and this contributes to the successful deployments of MPLS-based solutions in large scale networks. This type of experience does not yet exist in the SDN realm. With SDN, configuration complexity is reduced and potentially eliminated, as there are little or no traffic engineering configurations on the routers themselves. All or most of the configuration state exists in the logically centralized control plane. It may appear that implementing this capability in a logically centralized software layer should be simpler than deploying distributed MPLS protocols required in an MPLS-based solution. However, given the effort required in getting the SDN solution to initially function and operate, even at a basic level, it is clearly not a trivial undertaking. So, the question remains whether the increased complexity in the centralized control plane software offsets the configuration complexity in an MPLS solution. Additional operational and deployment experience with SDN traffic engineering solutions is required before the questions around operational complexity can be truly understood and answered.

Removing the MPLS signaling protocols from the network eliminates the associated router configuration complexity and eliminates any potential concern of router CPU or memory limitations. The network nodes are no longer responsible for maintaining protocol neighbor states, exchanging label allocations, maintaining LSDBs or TEDs, and other functions associated with distributed control plane protocols.

IPv6 Support

IPv6 support exists natively in OpenFlow so there should be no issue of supporting IPv4 and IPv6 in an SDN/OpenFlow-TE network. MPLS label support is also included in OpenFlow, which raises a question about whether MPLS labels could or should continue to be used in an SDN/OpenFlow-TE network. More on that specific topic later, but one question that needs to be discussed in an SDN/OpenFlow-TE solution is whether there is a need to continue to provide some form of encapsulated or tunneled data plane (as exists in MPLS solutions) to sufficiently aggregate traffic flows.

Need for Tunneling

Assuming that in an SDN traffic engineering solution that OpenFlow rules are pushed to every node in the network and that the network path is engineered in a "hop-by-hop" fashion, then scalability is a concern in any medium-to-large-scale network. If the traffic engineering is performed on a *per-flow* basis then this is not a feasible solution at Internet scale. So, the ability to aggregate traffic is required in both MPLS and SDN solutions. In MPLS, there is the Forwarding Equivalence Class (FEC) construct that results in mapping packets that are forwarded to the same IP destination next-hop into the same MPLS tunnel. For this discussion, let's assume that encapsulation and tunnel are inter-changeable terms. This tunneling capability is required to scale MPLS networks; in other words, to aggregate traffic flows to the same IP destination next-hop and that also require the same QoS treatment into the same tunnel. This mapping is only performed at the edge of the network and the core of the network simply forwards packets based on the MPLS label that is appended by the ingress router.

In an SDN/OpenFlow-TE solution, this encapsulation or tunneling capability would remain a requirement; otherwise it will never sufficiently scale in the core of any medium-to-large sized network. It is unreasonable to map packet flows at each hop in a large network—it simply will not scale in any medium-to-large network. One of the inventors of OpenFlow, Martin Casado of Nicira Networks, wrote a paper about OpenFlow and MPLS interaction and agreed that the ability to tunnel is required in order to scale a network of sufficient size. OpenFlow is too granular in that if there is no encapsulation or tunneling capability, then having to map each flow with an OpenFlow entry at every node in the network is not a deployable option (*http://yuba.stanford.edu/~casado/fabric.pdf*).

The bottom line is that there must be an "internal addressing" structure that is de-coupled from the "external addressing" schema to scale any network of this type and of sufficient size. In MPLS, these internal addresses are the MPLS labels. In SDN/OpenFlow-TE, the internal addresses could be private IP addresses (a.k.a. IP in IP encapsulation), or they could in the future continue to use MPLS labels. Does this provide additional context to the *hybrid network* we will likely see emerge over the next few years?

Failover Comparison

Another major area of differentiation between these solutions is how a rapid failover mechanism works when links or nodes in the topology fail. MPLS-based solutions have rapid recovery mechanisms using RSVP-based FRR. FRR is a widely deployed and very interoperable capability in MPLS networks. It can provide a sub-50 ms recovery capability, basically replacing the previous capability that carriers relied on with SONET-based networks. While it does add additional complexity to the network, the benefits of FRR are real and the trade-off in terms of additional complexity is widely deemed worthwhile. FRR capabilities are now available in non-MPLS networks, with IGP LFA (Loop Free Alternate) mechanisms, which is actually an FRR capability without the need for MPLS/RSVP-TE. SDN/OpenFlow-TE does not yet possess a capability that equates to MPLS FRR or IP LFA. This remains a glaring concern in SDN-based traffic engineered networks. While some of the basic machinery exists in OpenFlow to provide backup paths by adding additional entries in the flow table that are of a lower priority, the recovery times are not nearly equal to what FRR can provide. The OpenFlow group table option is being explored to see if it can provide improved fail-over recovery of OpenFlow paths.

In a simple OpenFlow example, assume an OpenFlow entry exists in the flow table that matches on a specific traffic type and specifies an outgoing interface that is on the shortest path as the forwarding action. Further assume there is a "secondary" OpenFlow entry in the flow table matching on the same traffic type but specifying a different outgoing interface. This second entry has a lower priority than the first entry and this allows for a pre-defined backup path. If the primary interface fails, the OpenFlow protocol does provide the ability of the local node to send a *Port Status Message* to the controller notifying it of the interface down event. It is now up to the SDN application running on the controller to react to this event and either delete the primary flow entry or change the priority of the entries so that the secondary entry gets promoted to become the primary flow entry. Traffic is then forwarded correctly out of the backup path. This is a time-consuming process and the propagation delay of the status message going from the local node to the controller will often exceed the desired 50ms threshold.

When factoring in the processing time of the SDN application and the propagation delay of sending a new OpenFlow rule or message back to the local node, it is clear this does not provide an equal ~50 ms recovery time. The round-trip transaction could take hundreds of ms or even several seconds, depending on the network topology and the location of the SDN controller(s). During that time period, traffic is black-holed as it is still being forwarded toward the interface that is no longer active. This area of SDN/OpenFlow-TE requires further innovation in order to provide roughly the same recovery times as MPLS FRR or IP LFA. The emerging OpenFlow group table may solve this problem. A capability on the local node to effectively monitor the active egress interface and remove it from eligibility in the flow table when it fails could mitigate the black-holing effect. This "local repair" action could be a temporary solution until the SDN application decides the ultimate solution in how the local flow table is updated to provide the failover capability. This would be similar to the functionality of MPLS FRR, where the local node performs the immediate recovery and local repair action to forward traffic over a backup or detour LSP while it signals back to the ingress router about the failure. The ingress router then determines the final failover path. In the meantime, the traffic is not black-holed due to the immediate re-route decision made by the local node.

Circuit Loading

One additional comment about the comparison of MPLS traffic engineering and SDN traffic engineering relates back to the ability to have a holistic global view of the networking resources. When real-time topological data is provided to the SDN application, the software can fully engineer the network to obtain the maximum utilization from the infrastructure. It is well known that in Google's G-scale SDN/OpenFlow-TE network, the inter-DC circuits are operating at nearly maximum utilization—understood to be nearly 98 or 99 percent utilization. This is unheard of in any other operational network. Since the traffic engineering application has a real-time global view of the topology, it can engineer the paths in this topology to obtain maximum utilization from the infrastructure.

In Google's inter-DC network they also possess full knowledge of the edge application traffic loading since they operate both the internal data center applications and the network connecting the data centers. This is not usually the case with a typical service provider; however, most large service providers also have traffic forwarding requirements between their own data centers. As cloud-scale, distributed data centers become the norm, what was traditionally Intra-DC East/West traffic is becoming Inter-DC East/West traffic. Most of this is internal enterprise traffic. So, while Internet-facing networks cannot be engineered to this level of utilization due to the lack of application loading knowledge in those networks, the service provider and enterprise that operate their own data centers could leverage this knowledge. In these service provider and enterprise inter-DC networks, if knowledge about Inter-DC East/West traffic loading is known then it should be possible to run those networks at very high levels of utilization. With MPLS-RSVP-TE solutions in inter-DC networks, even when the application data loading is known, it is still unprecedented to run those networks at anything near those levels of utilization. The reasons for this have been described and include the lack of a holistic global view, lack of centralized control, bin packing, and the lack of inferred predictability. MPLS/RSVP-TE networks continue to be over-provisioned to accommodate traffic being re-routed during network link or node failures.

One last note before moving on to related topics; this use case for using OpenFlow+SDN for traffic engineering is mostly tied to an Inter-DC network. This use case is not as applicable to Internet-facing or customer-facing networks—in those networks there is less knowledge on the expected data loads and applications traversing the network.

IETF PCE WG

The IETF Path Computation Element (PCE) WG is exploring protocols to enable a PCE-based architecture for the computation of paths for MPLS Traffic Engineered LSPs. In such an architecture, the path computation of the TE LSPs doesn't occur at the ingress / head-end Label-switched Edge Router (LER) like it does with traditional MPLS/RSVP-TE. The TE computation function would occur in a logically centralized element that is not physically co-located on the LER element. This sounds like SDN, doesn't it?

The WG has specified the PCE Communication Protocol (PCEP), which is kind of functionally similar to the OpenFlow protocol in an SDN architecture, if you squint hard enough. The PCE architecture is not intended to replace the distributed RSVP-TE signaling protocol; if it did, the TE LSP would need to be provisioned by the PCEP at each hop in the network. This would raise serious scalability concerns in an Internet-scale IP network. Many advantages described in the SDN/OpenFlow-TE model are present in a PCE-TE model, including the ability to view the network holistically and the ability to centrally provision paths with knowledge of this holistic view. This avoids or eliminates the scheduling and unpredictability issues in a traditional MPLS/RSVP-TE network.

The activities of this IETF WG are closely monitored by the industry, as it could provide a large proof point in the evolution of SDN architecture in general. The

Google SDN/OpenFlow-TE deployment, while extremely important as validation for SDN, is a limited deployment with a large budget (i.e., money and engineers). If PCE succeeds in supplanting the distributed computational element of MPLS/RSVP-TE, then this becomes a critical stage of evolution for SDN in these types of networks. The close comparisons from a high-level of SDN/OpenFlow-TE and PCE-TE should not be overlooked.

To conclude this section on SDN-based traffic engineering, a question again arises as to whether SDN/OpenFlow-TE could indeed replace the traditional MPLS/RSVP-TE architecture. Current thinking is this will not happen, as the distributed nature of RSVP-TE is required to scale a network of any significant size. In theory it is possible to provision TE paths in a large network from a logically centralized control function; however, the hop-by-hop provisioning is unnecessary when there are highly scalable and robust distributed protocols such as RSVP-TE. It appears likely that components of an SDN/OpenFlow-TE architecture could augment and be integrated with the traditional MPLS/RSVP-TE architecture. Such an architecture would likely leverage OpenFlow at the edge or ingress of the RSVP-signaled network. Basically, this would be a hybrid network.

At the PCE WG meeting at IETF 86 in early 2013, a draft was presented that specified providing control for Automatic Bandwidth (Auto-BW) LSP capabilities back to the distributed LER and LSR elements, even in a logically centralized PCE architecture. So, the question was raised about which functions are centralized and which functions are distributed. It seems unreasonable to centralize the computation element yet allow the distributed network elements to modify the parameters of the computed LSPs. This could easily result in race conditions and out-of-sync traffic engineered parameters.

Security, Network Access Control, DDoS

There have been interesting developments in the security space for the emerging OpenFlow/SDN architecture. One aspect of this new paradigm is the logical centralization of the managements and control planes. This can be deemed both good and bad from a security perspective. Good, in that the protection of the management and control planes may be more easily accomplished since they are logically centralized. Bad, in that this logical centralization becomes an obvious focal point for security attacks. However, this section is about the security-related use cases for an OpenFlow/SDN architecture—not whether this new paradigm is more or less secure than the current networking paradigm. That could be an entire book in itself.

Security, in general, in an OpenFlow and SDN world is just beginning to garner attention. As with most new networking technologies, security is often overlooked until late in the game. Recently, a brief security analysis of the OpenFlow v1.3 specification was documented and publicized in the IETF.

Doug Marschke, Jeff Doyle and Pete Moyer

[http://tools.ietf.org/html/draft-mrw-sdnsec-openflow-analysis-02]

One conclusion of the analysis is that the ONF should re-examine the security implications of the OpenFlow protocol. In addition, the IETF should continue to investigate the security aspects of the OpenFlow protocol and the SDN architecture in general. An important goal is for this emerging architecture to account for security as it is developed and deployed, rather than trying to "bolt on" security mechanism as an after-thought.

Having said this, the ONF is now taking a serious look at the security architecture of SDN and the OpenFlow protocol. It is very comforting to know that a standards organization such as the ONF is ensuring that security is not an after-thought.

Network Access Control

The basic Network Access Control (NAC) use case involves a solution that requires per-user authentication and then provides authorized computer access to network resources. The computer access is typically port-based; in other words, the computer can access the network via its Ethernet port and there is no additional level of granularity. Often, the MAC address of the Ethernet port becomes a permitted endpoint from a physical network perspective, while the individual user credentials may grant access to specific systems on the network based on username/password challenges.

The IEEE 802.1X standard defines this basic port-based form of network access control. This standard identifies the user machine as a "Supplicant" the first-hop access switch as the "Authenticator" and the backend software verifying the credentials of the user as the "Authentication Server." This is shown in Figure 6.

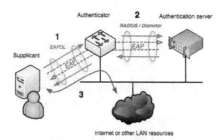

Figure 8. IEEE 802.1X Network Access Control Example
[http://en.wikipedia.org/wiki/IEEE_802.1X]

Campus network operators are considering using OpenFlow and SDN to augment this solution, or in some cases, as a complete replacement for this type of port-based NAC solution. Since OpenFlow can provide further granularities beyond just a port-based access model, it is appealing from a security perspective. An early use case for using a flow-based access model was Stanford's Ethane project, which focused on using a centralized controller to manage the security access policies. The controller determines whether a flow is authorized, based on the enterprise security policies, and if so, the controller pushes rules into the switches that allow the packets in the flow to be forwarded. This project was one of the early geneses of OpenFlow and SDN. The basic access model for Ethane is shown in Figure 7.

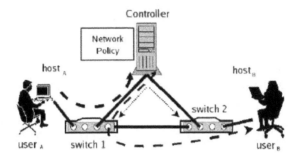

Figure 1: Example of communication on an Ethane network. Route setup shown by dotted lines; the path taken by the first packet of a flow shown by dashed lines.

Figure 9. Original Stanford ETHANE Network Access Control Example
[http://yuba.stanford.edu/ethane/pubs.html]

Network access control is a major issue in enterprise campus networks, particularly in higher education networks where the user population is often in the tens of thousands. Some of the recent investigations into using OpenFlow and SDN to provide this access control show that this model is similar to the Ethane model where, by default, none of the ports on an access switch permit access to the internal network. Initial flows are forwarded to the logically centralized OpenFlow controller(s). The software layer on this controller is fully integrated with the enterprise security solution, such as an AAA (Authentication, Authorization, and Accounting) solution. The AAA layer determines whether the flow is permitted and the OpenFlow controller then pushes an OpenFlow entry into the access switch, providing the granted access to the network. This is a more granular solution than the traditional port-based NAC solution. The OpenFlow entry could be based on the SRC MAC address, a DST MAC address, a wild-carded DST MAC address range, and other fields available in the OpenFlow specification, such as combining Layer 3 matching fields with Layer 2 fields to provide a very granular access model. The OpenFlow forwarding rules could force the user's traffic into a "quarantined network" for further analysis and authorization, or it could allow access to specific systems in the network. OpenFlow rules can even enforce which network devices and paths the user is authorized to traverse.

There are solutions being developed that are similar to what is described here, and it will be exciting to see these SDN solutions come to market.

DDoS Security Use Case

Another emerging SDN use case involving network security is related to DDoS mitigation. The basics of this use case can be applied to other appliances as well, such as IDS/IDP appliances. A basic requirement of a DDoS appliance is the ability to receive user traffic inline. An alternate architecture has the appliance(s) sitting off to the side, perhaps attached to an aggregation router. In this case, the router needs to forward or redirect traffic to the appliance. Currently, one method to force traffic towards a DDoS appliance (or IDS/IDP) is to use ACL + PBR configurations in the router. The DDoS appliance is attached to an aggregation or border router, and traffic is redirected into this DDoS appliance via policy configurations in the router. These PBR configurations override the RIB/FIB state in the router that would otherwise forward the traffic out another interface towards its intended destination. The DDoS appliance then receives the traffic and after inspection or treatment, the traffic is directed back into the network via routing policies or configurations in the appliance. The router then forwards traffic towards the intended destination, using its current RIB/FIB state. This is similar to the network service chaining use case; however, this use case includes a physical device attached to the aggregation router instead of a virtualized machine running on an appliance. But there is no reason this DDoS solution could not become virtualized and running as a VM on an x86 platform.

When SDN is applied to this use case, instead of complex and brittle PBR configurations in the router to force traffic into the security appliance, OpenFlow rules are used. The aggregation router connected to the security appliance is an OpenFlow enabled router and receives OpenFlow rules from the controller. There is software on the controller that, after the operator determines which traffic to force into the security appliance, pushes the OpenFlow rules into the router from the controller. This is another example of a router needing a "hybrid" capability, where it can use standard IP routing protocols in addition to OpenFlow rules. This is needed because the packets entering the router could be forwarded by the local IP RIB/FIB state or it can be forwarded by OpenFlow rules. Optionally, the aggregation router itself could discard the DDoS traffic using OF rules.

But how does the software on the controller determine which traffic to forward to the security appliance and when this forwarding should be implemented? The solution needs to be aware and intelligent enough to determine when a DDoS attack is in progress or potentially in progress, and it must be capable enough to implement rules that forward this suspected traffic into the proper security appliance for analysis or treatment. For this service to be effective, it requires a very dynamic capability. In addition, knowledge of the networking infrastructure utilization under normal loads and the associated traffic patterns must be benchmarked and known.

Once the operator has knowledge of the "normal" utilization of its links and devices, then traffic anomalies can provide alerts that indicate that a DDoS attack is potentially underway. A sampling capability, such as sFlow-RT, can be enabled in the network to sample traffic and provide network visibility to the network operator's network management systems. If traffic towards a particular customer or host spikes to unusual levels, then this is an anomaly that can signal to the operator that a DDoS attack is potentially underway. The security software can then determine which traffic needs to be redirected to a security appliance for analysis or treatment. This software instructs the controller(s) to push OpenFlow rules into the appropriate network devices so that the security appliance receives this suspected DDoS attack traffic. This same software can be used to instruct the controller to remove the OpenFlow rules from the appropriate network devices, based upon operator determination that the traffic is not a DDoS or otherwise malicious traffic.

In addition to monitoring the traffic loads and patterns for anomalies, specific parameters could be input into the application to determine which types of flows are malicious flows.

The OpenDaylight consortium is investigating an SDN DDoS solution similar to the one described here. Some of the same components described here are used in the OpenDaylight solution. Figure 10 shows the solution.

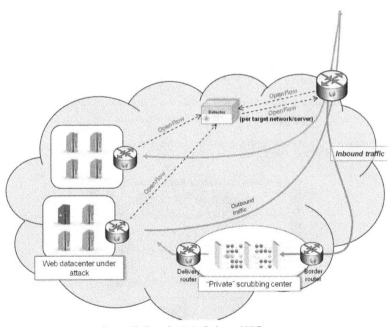

Figure 10. Open Daylight Defense4All Project
[https://wiki.opendaylight.org/view/Project_Proposals:Defense4All]

IXP Route Server

Other potential use cases for OpenFlow and SDN are being discussed in IETF and industry events such as various SDN conferences. At IETF 86 in March, 2013 an early glimpse at a possible use of OpenFlow in a Software Defined eXchange (SDX) point was presented.

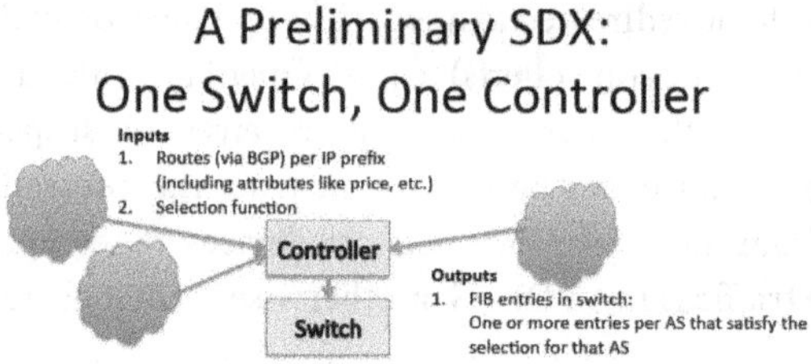

A Preliminary SDX: One Switch, One Controller

Inputs
1. Routes (via BGP) per IP prefix (including attributes like price, etc.)
2. Selection function

Controller

Outputs
1. FIB entries in switch: One or more entries per AS that satisfy the selection for that AS

Switch

Figure 11. Potential Software Defined Exchange Point Use Case 1
[http://www.ietf.org/proceedings/86/slides/slides-86-sdnrg-6]

Figure 11 illustrates a *very* preliminary use case, which leverages OpenFlow to push forwarding rules/entries into an OpenFlow-enabled switch. The learning of routes continues to leverage BGP; where the controller runs BGP to external BGP peers much like a traditional route-server in a traditional Internet Exchange Point (IXP). Potential advantages of using OpenFlow could be a more granular route selection capability, which equates to more granular forwarding entries in the OpenFlow switch. In other words, you can forward on a more granular decision process than just the best IP path. There is also the potential to have more dynamic policies in place in the controller to help determine which paths are the selected best paths.

While the actual utility of this use case remains in question, it suggests creative ways that OpenFlow can be used to provide real-life solutions.

A similar use case was presented at Apricot 2013.

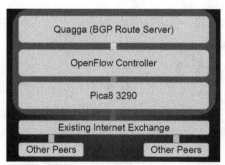

Figure 12. Potential Software Defined Exchange Point Use Case 2
[http://conference.apnic.net/__data/assets/pdf_file/0011/58934/project-cardigan_1361872406.pdf]

Figure 12 shows a use case that also leverages OpenFlow to push forwarding entries into a switch at an IXP. Both use cases are similar in that they continue to leverage BGP (they don't try to replace BGP), and they leverage OpenFlow to push the forwarding rules into the switch(es).

Yet another example of a similar use case presented at a public industry forum is shown in Figure 13.

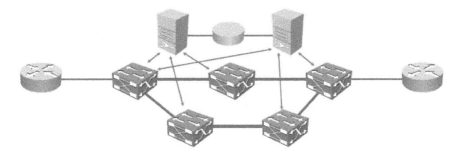

- Cluster of OpenFlow controllers
- Provisioning DB used for IP address information
- Phase 1: Edge functionality, *NORMAL* forwarding in core
- Phase 2: Core OpenFlow

Figure 13. Potential Software Defined Exchange Point Use Case 3

Figure 13 shows a cluster of OpenFlow controllers. The basic premise is the same with one major difference—this example does not use BGP to learn routes. Another interesting aspect of this example relates back to the discussion of an emerging "hybrid OpenFlow network." This use case leverages OpenFlow rules at the edge of the network while using "normal" forwarding in the core. A future phase would look at implementing OpenFlow for both the edge and the core. But the use of OpenFlow at the edge of networks to provide a very granular matching capability appears to be gaining some current mindshare. Why nail up each flow "hop-by-hop" with OpenFlow in all the nodes when there are robust and distributed protocols (such as MPLS) for doing that?

Summary

This section discussed several different use cases that leverage the OpenFlow protocol as part of an SDN-based solution. As expected, the SDN technologies and market place continues to evolve rapidly. Additional use cases will become relevant over time. Volume II of this book series will include additional use cases .

6

SDN - OpenFlow Use Cases

There are additional evolving use cases for Software Defined Networking that do not require the capabilities provided by the OpenFlow protocol. We have covered some SDN use cases that leverage or require the OpenFlow protocol, and now we will delve into some relevant use cases that are, for the most part, unrelated to the OpenFlow protocol. While the focus of this book is on SDN and OpenFlow, it would not be a fair assessment to ignore relevant SDN use cases that do not require OpenFlow.

SDN - OpenFlow Use Cases

While OpenFlow is one of the primary drivers that led to the SDN revolution we are currently experiencing; OpenFlow does not equate to SDN. In other words, SDN does not require OpenFlow. SDN includes a much larger market opportunity whereas OpenFlow is one key protocol within the SDN architecture. There are many use cases for SDN that are unrelated to the OpenFlow protocol.

As SDN is becoming more understood over time, many relevant use cases are emerging as engineers collaborate on offering new solutions within this emerging *software-defined* and *software-driven* world. These new solutions can solve existing network problems more efficiently and/or in a more scalable manner than the traditional solutions, or they can be solutions that offer innovative and agile network services. When thinking about which new services and opportunities are possible with SDN, NFV and NSC/SFC come immediately to mind. Keep in mind that SDN is the superset container whereas NFV, NSC/SFC and even OpenFlow are solutions, protocols, and functions within the larger SDN context.

This chapter will cover a few select use cases for SDN that do not require the OpenFlow protocol.

Network Virtualization

Here we go again talking about network virtualization. While we previously discussed how OpenFlow can be used in network virtualization solutions, additional technologies are required to truly virtualize a network. As we have said, OpenFlow is not intended to be a virtualization technology. The typical Ethernet LAN technology most often associated with virtualizing a network is the VLAN. The WAN virtualization section from Chapter 5 mentioned that while OpenFlow can be used in a virtualized WAN solution, OpenFlow did not actually provide the virtualization capability. VLANs are still leveraged in the LAN, and to a lesser extent the WAN, to provide the virtualization capability (although MPLS is typically associated with virtualized WANs). Many large issues remain when using VLANs, and they were discussed in Chapter 5, so we will not re-hash them here.

Data Center Virtualization

Due to the scalability and provisioning limitations with the traditional, large and flat Layer 2 networks that we have previously discussed, a new solution is emerging for providing this Layer 2 connectivity inside the DC. The requirement to have direct Layer 2 connectivity amongst many geographically dispersed systems remains today; and solving this requirement is becoming more problematic due to the high degree of server virtualization we are experiencing. While not all hosts and systems in large data centers require Layer 2 connectivity, this requirement does exist in many of the large data centers. VM mobility comes to mind as one of the drivers for this Layer 2 connectivity; in addition to the distributed nature of today's compute workloads. VMs are distributed across many different physical machines that may not be co-located; when these VMs need direct connectivity, a Layer 2 network must provide this connectivity. One of the basic premises behind server virtualization is resource allocation (i.e., the need to distribute VMs and associated workloads among the underused resources). If system administrators are forced to distribute these VMs and workloads to physical resources that are geographically adjacent to each other, this *dramatically* limits the deployment model. This would become a serious negative constraint in terms of the ability and efficiency of deploying services.

To provide this Layer 2 connectivity while avoiding the traditional issues with large broadcast domains, a Layer 2 logical network overlay is being deployed in today's multi-tenant data centers. This overlay requires some form of encapsulation or tunneling capability, instead of using traditional VLAN technology. The underlay network could be a Layer 3 enabled IP fabric of some sort (e.g., OSPF), or it could be a Layer 2 Ethernet fabric.

As we progress through the following DC use cases, keep in mind the requirements of today's cloud data centers: multi-tenancy, VM mobility, and the ability to meet these requirements with an agile, dynamic provisioning and orchestration capability that only software can provide.

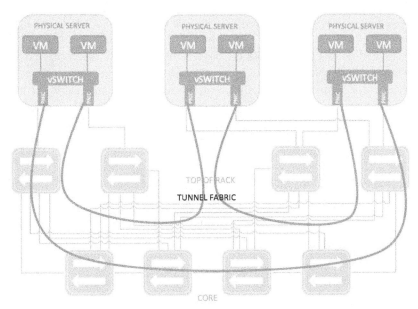

Figure I. Data Center Virtualization

VMware/Nicira NVP/NSX

Nicira Networks was very early to market in exploring and developing a Layer 2-over-Layer 3 overlay solution for the data center. VMware acquired Nicira in 2012 for over $1B. That was a massive *firing shot over the bow* to the industry in terms of where the data center architecture is heading and where the data center innovation is happening. The goal of NSX, like most of the other DC SDN applications now being developed, is to provide the ability to deploy a virtualized network in the DC at the same operational efficiency and dynamism as is available today with the deployment of virtualized servers. NSX provisions virtual Layer 2 switches (Open vSwitch) in the hypervisor layer to meet the applications connectivity needs. This connectivity creates a logical network overlay network that ties the various VMs together regardless of the geographic placement of the physical resources.

One result of this type of (new) logical network connectivity in the data center is that the *edge* of the data center network has moved into the server and no longer exists in the actual physical network infrastructure. The network edge has moved! It now exists in the server and is often referred to as the "server edge." As part of this type of new data center architecture, the logical network overlay is now decoupled from the physical network infrastructure. The network overlay consists of tunneling/encapsulation mechanisms in the hypervisor and the underlay could be a Layer 2 network or a Layer 3 network.

Initially, Nicira focused on GRE encapsulation to provide their tunneling/overlay capability, but eventually they proposed a new encapsulation to the IETF; the Stateless Transport Tunneling (STT) Protocol. Ethernet frames are encapsulated in the server before the frames reach the physical network, and the resulting overlay network is also labeled with a unique identifier that identifies each virtual network segment. This segmentation capability meets the multi-tenant requirements for cloud data centers.

[http://tools.ietf.org/html/draft-davie-stt-06]

Interestingly, prior to the Nicira acquisition VMware proposed its own overlay encapsulation called Virtual Extensible LAN (VXLAN) to provide a similar capability, while also overcoming the 4k VLAN limitation. More on VXLAN in a bit.

[https://tools.ietf.org/html/rfc7348]

The primary advantage of STT as compared to GRE, and the primary reason Nicira felt it was necessary to develop yet another encapsulation type, is that the STT encapsulation mechanism can leverage advanced capabilities in the Network Interface Card (NIC) to improve performance. Whenever any network device encapsulates a packet, it experiences a processing performance impact unless this encapsulation is done in hardware rather than in software. Modern router vendor products can now perform many different types of encapsulation for many different endpoints with little to no performance impact because they have moved this encapsulation mechanism into the data plane of the router's hardware. This is done in specialized application-specific integrated circuit (ASIC) and field-programmable gate array (FPGA) silicon. Since servers are not ASIC- or FPGA-based, the CPU of the server will be negatively impacted when performing this encapsulation capability and moreso when there are a lot of encapsulated endpoints in the server. STT can leverage the capabilities in modern NICs for performance gains vs. traditional encapsulation technologies such as GRE. This allows servers that use STT encapsulation to perform at a higher level than servers doing GRE encapsulation. Additionally, many server NICs today can perform TCP Segmentation Offload (TSO). STT is developed to take advantage of this TSO capability for improved performance.

VXLAN was developed by VMware to perform the same encapsulation capability needed to construct the Layer 2-over-Layer 3 overlay network. They felt the need to develop a new encapsulation as well. The VXLAN header structure is shown here.

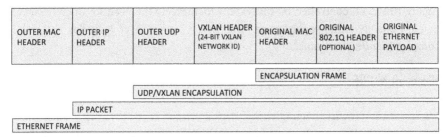

OUTER MAC HEADER	OUTER IP HEADER	OUTER UDP HEADER	VXLAN HEADER (24-BIT VXLAN NETWORK ID)	ORIGINAL MAC HEADER	ORIGINAL 802.1Q HEADER (OPTIONAL)	ORIGINAL ETHERNET PAYLOAD

ENCAPSULATION FRAME

UDP/VXLAN ENCAPSULATION

IP PACKET

ETHERNET FRAME

Figure 2: VXLAN Header

The basic premise remains the same whether using STT, VXLAN, or GRE – the encapsulation occurs in the hypervisor of the server and this provides a tunneling capability in order to provide Layer 2 logical connectivity over the underlay network (again, whether the underlay is Layer 2 or Layer 3). This tunneling capability meets the requirements of direct Layer 2 connectivity and multi-tenancy. It should be pointed out that VXLAN requires multicast to be enabled to forward BUM (Broadcast, Unknown Unicast, Multicast) traffic and some folks believe this requirement presents a deployment challenge in data centers.

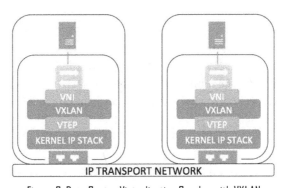

Figure 3: Data Center Virtualization Overlay with VXLAN

Note that we have not mentioned the OpenFlow protocol at all at this point. The reason is that it is not required in this type of solution. As we have pointed out, SDN does not equal OpenFlow. So, here is a prime example of a real-life SDN solution that is for the most part, unrelated to the OpenFlow protocol. Having said that, Nicira's solution does use the OpenFlow protocol to instantiate forwarding entries in the hypervisor that map MAC addresses into the appropriate tunnels. This is to eliminate the traditional mechanisms of MAC learning. VM and MAC address location information within the data center is used to populate the Layer 2 forwarding tables for the network overlay.

Again, this is all controlled by software, which meets the need for operational efficiency and dynamic provisioning. This Layer 2-over-Layer 3 overlay network is completely *software-defined*.

Microsoft NVGRE

Microsoft has its own tunneling/encapsulation variant, called Network Virtualization using Generic Routing Encapsulation (NVGRE). This specification is an IETF Internet Draft [http://tools.ietf.org/html/draft-sridharan-virtualization-nvgre-07].

The frame format is shown here.

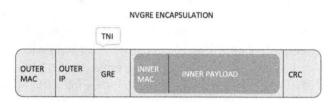

Figure 4: NVGRE Header

NVGRE includes a 24-bit Virtual Subnet Identifier (VSID) to distinguish amongs different customers in a multi-tenant network, and uses GRE to create the logical Layer 2 overlay network. NVGRE's purpose is basically identical to VXLAN and STT, in that it provides the tunneling capability to create the logical network overlay. Microsoft's Hyper-V Network Virtualization solution relies solely on NVGRE.

IBM DOVE

IBM has proposed its own tunneling/encapsulation mechanism. Do we have enough variants now, or do we need another? IBM's mechanism is called Distributed Overlay Virtual Ethernet (DOVE)) and like NVGRE, VXLAN and STT, it is their encapsulation mechanism for creating the logical network overlay. One difference between DOVE and VXLAN is that DOVE does not require an IP multicasting capability; however, it does use the same frame format as VXLAN. The elimination of the multicast requirement means this solution may be easier to deploy in DC environments; as these networks typically do not already have IP multicast deployed. It remains to be seen whether this alternate tunneling mechanism will receive a larger deployment base than VXLAN. As of this writing, VXLAN is still leading the way in terms of real deployments and mind-share.

IETF NVO3 WG

The IETF has jumped into the DC overlay solution space by creating a new WG called NVO3 (Network Virtualization Overlays). You can find the charter here: http://datatracker.ietf.org/wg/nvo3/charter/. Directly from the charter -

The purpose of the NVO3 WG is to develop a set of protocols and/or protocol extensions that enable network virtualization within a data center (DC) environment that assumes an IP-based underlay. An NVO3 solution provides layer 2 and/or layer 3 services for virtual networks enabling multi-tenancy and workload mobility, addressing the issues described in the problem statement (including management and security), and consistent with the framework previously produced by the NVO3 WG.

As with all of these solutions, providing a multi-tenancy capability is a primary driving requirement. NVO3 will not recommend a single tunneling/encapsulation mechanism but rather will focus on the higher level architecture needed to provide the network overlay solutions, both within a single DC and across multiple DCs. This WG is very active at all the IETF meetings and so far has had very good representation from network operators and network equipment vendors. It is quickly becoming the "battleground" where operators and vendors hash out the details of the future DC network requirements and architecture. If you are not yet following the activities within this WG, we highly recommended you start doing so if you desire to remain up to speed with what's happening in this space.

Some key aspects of their current work are identifying and producing the following: a problem statement, a framework for DC network virtualization, a requirements document and gap analysis, and an initial high-level architecture proposal. One additional thing worth mentioning with NVO3 is that MPLS encapsulation has often been discussed in this WG, in addition to the other encapsulation types discussed here. This brings an interesting angle to the entire DC network architecture conversation. Some folks will argue that since MPLS has long provided the WAN virtualization capability (e.g., MPLS VPNs), why shouldn't this technology be extended into the DC? This will be an interesting debate to watch. More on this topic in the next section when we discuss WAN Virtualization.

Before we move on, it's worth pointing out that there are now additional encapsulations being proposed in the NVO3 WG.

[http://www.ietf.org/id/draft-gross-geneve-00.txt]
[https://datatracker.ietf.org/doc/draft-quinn-vxlan-gpe/]

This proves the point that we are still somewhat early in the deployments of data center SDN virtualization solutions. The industry still has not agreed on which virtualization frame format to standardize on; even if it's selecting two to provide a choice. I guess one can ask the question, "Are we done yet?", when it comes to encapsulation types?

ONF and ODL

It wouldn't be fair to exclude the ONF and ODL when discussing data center virtualization. Both the ONF and the ODL are also pursuing recommendations and solutions in this space. There is clearly a lot of industry interest in providing the right solution(s) for data center virtualization and this area of innovation will remain quite active for the foreseeable future. And who said that networking got boring?

WAN Virtualization

It is well known that MPLS technologies provide WAN virtualization solutions in most of today's SP networks and in a growing number of large enterprise networks. It is also well known that previously in the WAN of SP networks, ATM was the technology of choice for providing virtualization of the network. This virtualization has long provided a multi-tenancy solution for the WAN and this multi-tenancy requirement has now been extended into the data center. In the WAN, ATM (and Frame Relay) have been replaced by MPLS for well over a decade now. MPLS technology provides virtualization functionality at both Layer 2 and Layer 3. Layer 2 capabilities are provided by Pseudo-Wire Emulation Edge-to-Edge (PWE3) and Virtual Private LAN services (VPLS). Layer 3 capabilities are provided by BGP/MPLS VPNs.

A question often comes to mind when discussing how SDN might impact MPLS; that is, will OpenFlow replace these well-known and widely deployed MPLS technologies for virtualizing the WAN? That question was discussed in Chapter 5. If you have already forgotten the current thinking towards answering that question, it's that OpenFlow will not replace MPLS in the WAN for providing virtualized networks. It will likely integrate with existing MPLS networks but it should not be viewed as a replacement for MPLS. OpenFlow and MPLS do not solve the same problems. This section will not focus so much on whether SDN technologies can or will replace the currently deployed MPLS technologies for WAN virtualization; it will focus instead on how SDN technologies might augment and/or interwork with the currently deployed MPLS networks.

While some marketing material may pop up on the Internet, if you do a search on "WAN Virtualization with SDN," there is actually very little industry effort to provide yet another virtualization technology in the WAN that is considered "SDN." Other than MPLS, that is. There is little incentive or movement in the industry to attempt to replace MPLS as the de-facto WAN virtualization technology. Why fix something that is not broken? While it can be argued that MPLS is a complex technology and that there are some provisioning and deployment challenges in operating large MPLS networks, there is no real evidence that MPLS does not provide a sufficient WAN virtualization service that meets the requirements of the largest SP operators. The current belief is that MPLS will continue to dominate the WAN infrastructure. So, why are we even discussing this topic as part of an SDN book? Well, what is important to discuss is how to integrate the existing virtualized MPLS WAN with the emerging virtualized data center LAN. One simple answer to this problem is to implement some sort of "gateway" function that sits between the traditional MPLS WAN and the new SDN-based virtualized data center. This gateway maps the virtualized data center network constructs to the virtualized MPLS WAN instances. For example, this gateway function could terminate the data center virtualized segments (e.g., VXLAN, NVGRE) and map that traffic into an MPLS Virtual Routing and Forwarding (VRF) instance that exists in a traditional MPLS Provider Edge (PE) router. Alternately, this gateway function could keep the data center construct intact and tunnel this encapsulated traffic into an MPLS Label Switched Path (LSP). Both approaches are valid and both approaches are being examined in various standards bodies and communities.

To properly integrate the WAN with the virtualized data center network, there are two classes of gateway functions being developed: one where the DC overlay network must also provide external connectivity to the Internet and/or external Enterprise network (e.g., hybrid cloud) and another where the DC overlay network must also provide connectivity to an existing WAN MPLS network.

An additional question comes up on whether it is feasible to have this gateway functionality implemented purely in software on a standardized hardware platform, or is a specialized network device required to implement the gateway functionality. Today some early software-based solutions exist for providing this type of gateway; however, scalability and performance of this approach are currently questionable and a cause for some concern. Some folks will argue that a physical specialized device is required for performance reasons but this flies in the face of the current thinking and trends toward NFV. It is too early to say whether this gateway functionality will ultimately be implemented by a specialized network device, or as a software service residing on "white box" or bare-metal x86 machines.

Translation Gateway

The more popular approach currently being deployed is to provide a translation capability between the virtualized DC network and the virtualized MPLS WAN network. A simpler version of this type of gateway is providing Internet or other external access to the tenants of a virtualized DC network. VXLAN Tunnel End

Point (VTEP) is one such example for VXLAN-based DC overlay networks. In other words, terminating each of the virtualized DC networks and providing external IP access. This is not much different from how legacy VLAN-based DC segments are terminated in a router, and how the original Ethernet payload is then encapsulated in IP and routed toward its destination. Instead of terminating VLANs, the gateway now terminates VXLAN, NVGRE, or STT segments. There is nothing really special or different here except that this is new functionality being deployed in the data center. Some of these implementations are purely being done in software, while others are being done in hardware devices.

Where it gets interesting is when the tenants of a virtualized DC segment need connectivity to tenants within an MPLS VPN in the WAN. Now the virtualized DC segment needs to be terminated and the traffic needs to be transported to one or more MPLS PE routers in the WAN. The gateway node requires knowledge of which MPLS VRF instance to map the virtual DC segments traffic into.

Some of the emerging solutions for virtualizing the DC network actually involve extending MPLS technology from the WAN into the DC, instead of terminating and/or translating in a gateway device. This may make sense since MPLS is so widely deployed and well understood by most network operators. Scalability becomes an obvious concern, since each of the many hypervisors in the DC network could now behave in a similar manner as traditional MPLS PE routers. MPLS VPN WANs are often already exhibiting scaling problems; can you imagine adding an additional hundred or more PE nodes into such a network? It is an interesting use case, however; and there are implementations being developed. Doing this in a manner that does not require the server hypervisor to support all the functionality of a traditional PE router is the hurdle that needs to be overcome. Can you imagine servers having to run an IGP, BGP, and an MPLS signaling protocol?

Tunneling Gateway

This approach isn't being pursued as actively as the translation approach. The concept of this approach is similar to Layer 2 MPLS VPNs and how those solutions encapsulate VLAN tagged frames into LSPs for transport over the WAN. In the emerging DC model, a VXLAN, NVGRE or STT encapsulated packet would be transported in tact over an MPLS WAN. The MPLS label is popped off at the egress router (actually at the penultimate router, due to penultimate hop popping) and out comes the original VXLAN, NVGRE, or STT encapsulated packet.

While this "double tunneling" concept may at first appear to be a bad idea, it is really no different than Q-in-Q, PBB, and how MPLS VPNs are transported over MPLS TE networks (e.g., MPLS label stacking).

To summarize this section, the SDN solutions being developed today are not intended to replace the MPLS technologies that are currently deployed. MPLS will remain the WAN virtualization technology of choice for the foreseeable future. However, solutions are being developed to augment the existing and deployed MPLS solutions.

The area most relevant to WAN virtualization is how the MPLS-enabled WAN will integrate with the emerging virtualized DC network. This is an emerging area of work being undertaken by various standards bodies and communities, particularly within the IETF. It is very early to say how the industry will solve this problem; however, there is quite a bit of smart brain power being put into this area so it looks very promising.

WAN Routing

There are some very interesting developments in the area of SDN applications for WAN routing, and they do not require the use of the OpenFlow protocol. These developments are not intended to replace the currently deployed WAN routing solutions, nor are they intended to invent yet another WAN routing protocol. They are being developed to augment the existing WAN routing deployments. The intention is to augment the routing domain with software-defined and software-driven enhancements.

Some folks currently think that the developments in this area are more towards augmenting the provisioning and operational aspects of routing (and traffic-engineering); however, they are much more than that. For example, these developments may not enhance or replace existing provisioning tools such as NetConf. We will discuss a few of the more important developments in this area, how they apply and relate to the SDN trend, and their impacts to deployed networks. It will become clear that these developments are evolutionary and not revolutionary when it comes to WAN routing and traffic engineering. These work today, so why try to replace them? Instead, let's focus on enhancing them in an evolutionary way.

IETF I2RS

We touched on the IETF I2RS WG in Chapter 5. This is a good place to go a bit deeper on this subject as it relates to the SDN-enhanced WAN routing domain. The I2RS efforts are examining a way to standardize one or more software interfaces, basically a routing API, which programs state into and extracts state out of the RIBs of deployed routers. It is not intended to replace the deployed routing systems; but rather, it intends to provide a more functional, dynamic, and most importantly, *standardized* ability to inject state into the routing domain. It will be equally capable of extracting routing state from the routing domain. This extracted routing state can be fed into intelligent software applications that can then determine whether the routing domain and topology should be modified or optimized. This goes back to the previous discussion on the need for network analytics. Some legitimate reasons for modifying the routing state of a network could be to provide more optimal routing paths, to provide an efficient load-balancing capability, or to inject a priori backup paths into the routing domain. Those are just a few examples.

One prime difference with the I2RS architecture from the existing routing domain architecture is that all the processes associated with the current routing domain are embedded (e.g., co-located) in the deployed routing elements themselves. Each router runs multiple processes to individually determine its proper forwarding state. This creates a massively distributed routing domain. This distributed routing domain is the key reason the Internet has been able to continue to scale. I2RS intends to augment this existing distributed routing domain with a real-time, standardized interface into the routing elements; both in the control and the management plane.

Some of the use cases currently being discussed relate to the network routing topology and to network service chaining (NSC). NSC was discussed in Chapter 5, so we will focus on the network topology use case here.

Real-time network topology information is required for efficient and proper traffic engineering, capacity planning, network optimization, and other reasons. Today, applications and back-office systems that can gather this type of information from the routing system are often proprietary and do not interoperate. Each network vendor has their proprietary mechanisms for gathering network topology information from their devices and for provisioning and modifying the network topology in their devices. SNMP, CLI, and even NetConf all have proprietary elements and this makes it *extremely* difficult and inefficient for any network operator to deploy and efficiently operate a medium to large multi-vendor network. Multi-vendor networks are deployed today, but only after a great deal of modification to the control and management systems to make the new vendors' equipment operational. In large Tier 1 networks it is currently assumed that to integrate a new network vendor would require months of planning, testing, and integration and the cost to properly modify, update, or replace existing software systems could run into the millions of dollars. Yes, millions! A new approach is clearly needed.

I2RS will provide a common, standards-based topology view to these applications and back-office systems. Again, this interface is bi-directional. It will provision new topology state *and* extract topology state. It will do this by interacting directly with the RIBs of the deployed routers, using a common API. It is much more than a glorified version of NetConf.

Routing Optimization in I2RS

Optimization of the routed topology is an ongoing process that is typically handled by the distributed algorithms running on the deployed network elements. There is no global view of this topology and the currently defined algorithms do not take into account many aspects of the overall routing topology. One simple example is that an IGP is not aware of the actual traffic load on a link; it simply calculates a shortest path tree based on the assigned or calculated metric of the link. While there are limited tools and mechanisms available today to augment and optimize the IGP topology, these tools are mostly off-line and do not provide much of a real-time optimization capability. In addition to their limited capabilities, these tools are usually proprietary. I2RS also intends to solve these problems.

Directly related to routing optimization, the PCE WG in the IETF is developing protocols and solutions to enhance the MPLS-based traffic-engineered networks. PCE was covered in the Traffic Engineering section of Chapter 5.

Network Service Optimization in I2RS

When a new network service is provisioned in the routing domain, real-time topology information is not being examined or considered to determine how to properly and efficiently provision that service. Once a standardized system is in place that provides a real-time view into the globally optimized network topology, the next logical step when provisioning new network services is to leverage this topology information. That's just too obvious isn't it?

One simple example is when a new VPN service is provisioned and "overlayed" onto the existing network topology. Shouldn't the VPN overlay take into account the current network topology state? This would alleviate the current mode of operation when a new VPN service is provisioned; which often results in causing unexpected congestion in the network since it is not provisioned in such a manner as to take full advantage of the available network capacity. Existing customers are often impacted when new customers are added. This is clearly broken. I2RS will allow these new network services to be provisioned without impacting existing customers since the provisioning and orchestration system has full knowledge of the current network state. That's the current thinking anyway.

Operational Optimization in I2RS

Similar to the previous description that will provide an efficient ability to provision new services, the I2RS network topology system can also help with the operational aspects of managing and troubleshooting the routing domain. Having the ability to view and query the network topology in real-time will rapidly reduce the time it takes to identify and correct network routing problems. Confusion often abounds during times of operational stress associated with an ongoing network outage. If the current network state and topology are unknown and cannot be queried or verified, then it becomes extremely difficult to identify, localize, and correct the problem. The value of an I2RS supplied network topology system should be evident when it comes to the operational aspects of managing an IP network.

Network Functions Virtualization

NFV was briefly covered in previous chapters but we will cover it in more detail here. There are many associated use cases to discuss in the realm of NFV and we will cover some of the more interesting ones.

Before diving into NFV, it is worth taking a step back to identify the relationship NFV has to SDN. Similar to OpenFlow, NFV is a component within the SDN umbrella. Just as OpenFlow does not equate to SDN, NFV does not equate to SDN. As is often the case, there are clear software-defined aspects within the NFV context that makes an NFV conversation soon evolve into an SDN conversation.

The formalized NFV push was initiated by service providers in the 2012-2013 timeframe and the work is being driven out of ETSI. This important activity continues to gain rapid interest among both service providers and network vendors. The second version of the ETSI NFV white paper was released in late 2013 and a third version was released in 2014. The requirements, use cases, and architectural framework continue to expand. NFV is rapidly becoming the dominant SDN related topic of discussion amongs the largest service providers. These service providers are aggressively driving their network vendors to rapidly facilitate the development of open and software-based, virtualized network functions that run on open compute platforms (e.g., x86); as opposed to the ongoing deployment of these functions on specialized and proprietary network appliances.

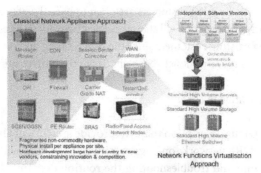

Figure 5: Vision for NFV
[http://portal.etsi.org/nfv/nfv_white_paper2.pdf]

One ETSI NFV document that is important to discuss is the one describing the various potential use cases for NFV. The relevant use cases will continue to evolve but the current target list includes:

1. Network Functions Virtualization (NFV) Infrastructure as a Service
2. Virtual Network Function (VNF) as a Service
3. Virtual Network Platform (NVP) as a Service
4. VNF Forwarding Graphs
5. Virtualization of Mobile Core Network and IMS
6. Virtualization of Mobile Base Stations
7. Virtualization of the Home Environment
8. Virtualization of CDNs
9. Fixed Access NFV

As you can see, this list of use cases covers a wide range of network functions and services. A few of these are worthy of mentioning here.

NFV Infrastructure as a Service (NFVIaaS)

Not all service providers have the resources to deploy and maintain physical infrastructures around the globe. The ability to remotely deploy and run Virtualized Network Functions (VNF) inside a virtualized network infrastructure, *provided as a service by another service provide*r, permits a service provider to extend its reach and coverage area and provide services in an efficient manner to its global customers. In other words, the ability for a Tier 1 service provider to offer its NFV infrastructure as a service to other Tier 2 or Tier-3 service providers offers an additional value-add commercial service offering for that provider.

VNF as a Service (VNFaaS)

Rather than offering a virtualized network infrastructure as a service, a service provider can offer a virtualized network function as a service. This is a granular and specific virtualized function provided by the service provider. This eliminates the need for the service provider and/or enterprise customer to deploy specialized hardware devices for each type of network function required. Consider the case of providing MPLS VPNs as a service. This is a very common service provider capability that requires a large quantity of specialized hardware devices such as Customer Edge (CE) routers, Provider Edge (PE) routers, and Provider core (P) routers. If the CE and/or PE functions can be virtualized onto standardized hardware, this equates to a compelling CAPEX and OPEX savings.

Another simple example is the current deployment model for network firewalls. These are deployed in high numbers on specialized and proprietary hardware devices. If the firewall functionality can be virtualized and run on standardized commercial hardware, this equates to a direct CAPEX and OPEX savings.

Network functions that are possible candidates for virtualization are:

1. CE and PE routers
2. Broadband Remote Access Servers
3. Firewalls
4. Deep Packet Inspection devices
5. Intrusion Detection Systems
6. Server Load Balancers

Virtualization of CDNs (vCDN)

Specialized content delivery networks are widely deployed to serve the growing demand for real-time and high quality video streams. Customers demand instant gratification when they initiate a request to watch a particular video stream. This instant gratification applies to most consumer services that are now offered over the network. Service providers not only want to meet this instant demand to provide service, they also want to eliminate any inefficient delivery of these services, especially streaming video since this type of traffic consumes an inordinate amount of network capacity. CDNs solve both of these requirements.

The CDN cache nodes are typically deployed on specialized physical hardware appliances or as software on dedicated physical servers. The CDN solution also requires specialized CDN controller nodes, in addition to the cache nodes. Virtualizing these functions into a virtual CDN service equates to a direct CAPEX and OPEX savings. This use case resembles the VNF as a service use case.

NFV is a huge topic to discuss and it will be a primary component of Volume II of this SDN book series.

Summary

This chapter focused on SDN use cases that do not include the OpenFlow protocol. Although this book is based on SDN + OpenFlow, it would not be a fair assessment of the SDN market place if the use cases that do not require OpenFlow are ignored.

A majority of the innovation in SDN-based solutions continues to happen in the data center networking space. Logical network overlays that provide Layer 2 connectivity among a set of geographically dispersed VMs is a prime area of ongoing innovation. There are many overlapping solutions in this space, each with different encapsulation and tunneling mechanisms. It will be very interesting to see how this plays out in the market place. As has been said many times with previous competing or overlapping technologies – the market will ultimately decide.

The IETF and other standards bodies, such as ONF and ETSI, are developing SDN-based architecture frameworks and solutions. These solutions are based on the relevant use cases and problem areas that network providers are experiencing.

Volume II of this book series will have many updates in this exciting and rapidly evolving SDN marketplace!

7

Other Things SDN

This chapter covers some of the many "other things SDN." While this book focuses on OpenFlow, SDN and their associated technologies, this chapter focuses on other important technologies that some might argue are also SDN, or not. The primary goal of this chapter is to provide the reader with a wider perspective of this emerging software-defined paradigm. A secondary goal is to eliminate some confusion surrounding the associated technologies and to help determine whether these technologies are or are not a form of software-defined networking.

What else might be considered "SDN"?

The SDN buzzword has clearly overtaken the "cloud" buzzword of previous years. Soon it will be "Software Defined Everything." SDN still means many things to many different people and is often mistaken for anything cloud, software-defined, software-driven or (now) NFV related. We have covered the SDN definition, applications, and use cases up to this point and we will now pivot to what else might be considered SDN (or not).

SDN via APIs

All SDN architectures and solutions require Application Programming Interfaces (API). APIs provide the primary programmatic and orchestration capabilities of all things SDN. These APIs must be open; they cannot be vendor-specific, else that negates the industry movement towards open networking. Often, open networking and SDN are assumed to be mutually inclusive. This volume discussed many of these APIs and the ensuing volumes of this series will continue to discuss APIs. New and emerging APIs will hit the market in the coming years. Many different industry bodies, such as ONF and IETF, are very active in the creation of APIs that provide programmatic or orchestration capabilities. APIs are considered the "glue" that ties the layers of an open SDN architecture together.

SDN via Overlays

We have also discussed overlay networks in this volume. Often, people think that DC overlays = SDN. However, overlays are only one category of DC SDN solutions. Overlays do not provide programmatic control of the forwarding layer in the DC network; this is an area that OpenFlow could potentially fill. The DC underlay network cannot be overlooked when considering the SDN paradigm. The underlay network also requires programmatic control and simplified provisioning.

The DC overlay space is fairly well understood at this point; however, the solutions are not yet finalized and the NVO3 WG in the IETF is an example of the state of flux in this space. But an area of emerging interest is the WAN overlay network and its implications to SDN. MPLS is the common WAN overlay technology and will continue to be for some time. There are SDN-like programmatic and optimization capabilities being actively discussed and created for MPLS to move this technology more towards a software-defined architecture. The PCE WG in IETF is one example of this.

Open SDN

As mentioned, open networking and SDN should be mutually inclusive technologies. The authors of this book do not believe you can have SDN unless the technologies, protocols and APIs involved are based on open standards. Furthermore, these solutions could very well be based on open source software. It is not yet well understood how open source will ultimately impact the SDN evolution and how well the market will deploy open source SDN solutions. This will be a very interesting area to keep track of!

Open SDN holds tremendous promise. To really get there, a comprehensive re-engineering of networking needs to take place. The networking era of closed and vertically integrated solutions needs to evolve towards open and horizontally integrated solutions. Each layer of the overall SDN solution should be replaceable with another vendor's offering. In other words, each layer should be interchangeable. The DC underlay network, the DC overlay network, the network operating system, the SDN controller platform, the SDN orchestration platform, and all the applications that sit on those platforms should be replaceable. Open APIs provide the glue holding all these layers together, which is why the evolution towards open APIs is so critical to the eventual success of SDN.

Data Center Orchestration

The Software Defined Data Center (SDDC) is becoming a more common phrase as we progress through the cloud and SDN paradigms. Data center orchestration is closely related to SDN, although not entirely the same thing. SDN clearly involves orchestration but it can also involve a fair amount of control and data plane programmability. For example, DC orchestration often does not involve or require OpenFlow support for programmability. Orchestration provides network service agility and is typically focused on reducing OPEX by flexibly simplifying operations and provisioning. In contrast, SDN can result in reduced OPEX and CAPEX, particularly when we talk about NFV in the SDN context.

OpenStack

Directly from the OpenStack website [https://www.openstack.org/software/]:

OpenStack is a cloud operating system that controls large pools of compute, storage, and networking resources throughout a datacenter, all managed through a dashboard that gives administrators control while empowering their users to provision resources through a web interface.

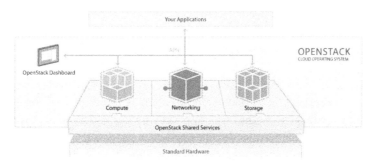

Figure 1: OpenStack Architecture

OpenStack is clearly focused on the Software Defined Data Center. The networking component of OpenStack (Neutron) is relatively basic at this time, as compared to the computing component, although its capabilities are growing with each distribution release. The OpenStack community is actively innovating in all aspects of DC orchestration, and if you are able to attend one of the OpenStack Summits, this becomes very obvious. Open source continues to gain wide industry adoption and this particular community appears to be growing in leaps and bounds.

Every networking vendor has OpenStack plugins available for their gear. While these plugins work with a specific vendor's gear, the intent of OpenStack is to offer vendor-neutral plugins to the marketplace. So, to be a good citizen, a vendor that implements a functional capability for OpenStack should make that capability work with other vendor's gear; it should not be proprietary. It will be interesting to see how this evolves over time, as some traditional networking vendors continue to choose to do things in a closed manner. The entire open source community effort (e.g., OpenStack, OpenDaylight) intends to release customers from any single vendor's lock-in strategy. Open source is really influencing customer buying decisions, which in turn influences vendor strategies and road maps.

CloudStack

CloudStack is another open source effort for DC orchestration. CloudStack was originally developed by Cloud.com, which was then acquired by Citrix. Citrix donated CloudStack to the Apache Software Foundation in 2012, under which it continues to operate. CloudStack is not nearly gaining the same industry acceptance as OpenStack.

OpenDaylight

OpenDaylight operates under the open source LINUX Foundation, similar to OpenStack. The OpenDaylight SDN Platform (ODP) intends to become the industry "de facto" SDN controller platform; and is well on its way toward this goal. There are key differentiators between OpenDaylight and OpenStack that are worth clarifying here.

OpenDaylight is not solely focused on DC orchestration, as OpenStack is. While there are some recent OpenStack plugin submissions that help provision and automate Inter-DC connectivity, the majority of the OpenStack community involvement focuses on the Software Defined DC. In addition, OpenDaylight does not provision or orchestrate computer or storage resources as does OpenStack.

OpenDaylight has an SDN controller at its central architecture. Control does not always equate to orchestration. Also significantly different is that the ODP fully leverages the OF protocol (v1.0 & v1.3) as one of its prime southbound APIs.

Taking a quick look at the projects under the OpenDaylight Developer Wiki provides an overview of the networking functions they are targeting. It is quite a large list of wide ranging projects that cover many aspects of networking.

[https://wiki.opendaylight.org/view/Main_Page]

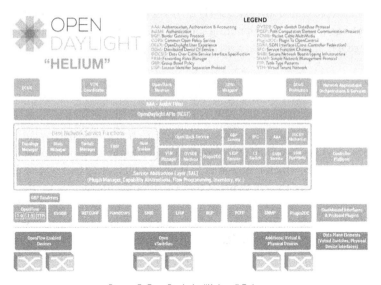

Figure 2: OpenDaylight "Helium" Release

So, OpenDaylight serves up programmatic and orchestration capabilities for a wide range of networking functions while OpenStack primarily serves up orchestration for the SDDC.

Open Networking Foundation (ONF)

One question that might come to mind is: Does ONF control the emerging SDN architecture? Since the ONF is responsible for the OF protocol specification (and didn't the OF protocol lead to the birth of SDN?), one might initially believe that ONF is perhaps also responsible for SDN. However, this is far from the case. The SDN paradigm is now an industry wide effort and no one organization could possibly be in charge of this emerging architecture.

The ONF is a user-driven organization dedicated to the promotion and adoption of SDN through open standards development. While the focus of ONF is around the OpenFlow protocol specification, it has branched out into other areas of SDN. An example of this is the "IETF-like" Working Group (WG) methodology that the ONF has adopted. Take a quick peek at some of the current Working Groups in the ONF:

[https://www.opennetworking.org/working-groups/working-groups-overview]

It is clear that the ONF is at the forefront of the emerging SDN paradigm; however, they are one amongst many industry standards bodies that are spurring rapid innovation and adoption of SDN technologies.

While we covered OpenFlow extensively in this book (after all, it is the primary focus of this volume!), its also worth noting some of the other interesting activities in the ONF. The ONF has worked on a specification called OF-Config.

[https://www.opennetworking.org/sdn-resources/onf-specifications/openflow-config]

There is a recognized need for additional configuration and management capabilities, beyond what OpenFlow can provide. This led to the development of this OF-config specification, which is now at v1.2. However, OF-config isn't widely used nor supported in many of the OF switches that are shipping today.

RFC 7047, The Open vSwitch Database Management Protocol is the more widely deployed option instead of OF-config. OVSDB was initially created by Nicira as part of Open vSwitch (OVS). The intent is to create an open management protocol for OVS.

One additional item worth mentioning in the ONF context is the ongoing work in the Forwarding Abstraction WG (FAWG) around Table Type Patterns (TTP). The FAWG was created to address the slow adoption of the OF specification in available hardware silicon. This work describes the switch level abstractions that is required to get wider adoption of the OF protocol.

Internet Engineering Task Force (IETF)

All or most of the standardized protocols in use today emerged from within the IETF. Without the IETF, the Internet as we know it today would not exist. This is not an over statement. While the IETF has traditionally focused on Internet protocols and technology, this standards body has now fully embraced the SDN revolution. While SDN cannot be standardized in itself, as it is an overall architecture, many aspects of SDN can become industry standards. The IETF has recently been very active in many of the protocols and technologies that fall under the SDN umbrella.

Interface to the Routing System (I2RS)

Emerging in 2013, the Interface to the Routing System (I2RS) is a new IETF WG that is focused on SDN-like technologies for IP routed networks. Directly from the WG charter:

I2RS facilitates real-time or event driven interaction with the routing system through a collection of protocol-based control or management interfaces. These allow information, policies, and operational parameters to be injected into and retrieved (as read or by notification) from the routing system while retaining data consistency and coherency across the routers and routing infrastructure, and among multiple interactions with the routing system. The I2RS interfaces will co-exist with existing configuration and management systems and interfaces.

It is envisioned that users of the I2RS interfaces will be management applications, network controllers, and user applications that make specific demands on the network.

So, it is clear that this is an SDN-like charter, and the I2RS will ultimately provide a standardized interface into the routed networking devices (i.e., Layer 3 routers). One thing worth pointing out is the specific mention of a model that will "… co-exist with existing configuration and management systems and interfaces." This is a "hybrid network" model that has been mentioned several times in this book, as opposed to the "purist" ONF perspective and definition of SDN. The I2RS will not remove all control and management plane functionality from the network devices, as is the intent of the ONF SDN model.

A few other things worth mentioning is the call out in the charter of an interface into the RIB of networking devices and explicit exclusion of an interface into the FIB of networking devices. Directly related to RIB interaction, the BGP protocol is also specifically mentioned in the charter as a discussion topic. Could a BGP version 5 be in the works as an (un)intentional outcome of I2RS? Thats doubtful, but the ultimate outcome of this WG is yet unclear.

The work and use cases of this WG are still under definition but this is a prime WG to be following within the IETF to see how Internet-wide SDN-like technologies and protocols progress.

Path Computation Element (PCE)

The PCE WG has been previously mentioned but we'll cover it again briefly here. This WG is not new in IETF, having been chartered in 2005. Yet, it gained relatively little excitement and activity until recently. The SDN era we are experiencing drove new activity into the WG and it is now another very relevant SDN-like WG within the IETF. The charter is listed here:

The PCE Working Group is chartered to specify the required protocols so as to enable a Path Computation Element (PCE)-based architecture for the computation of paths for MPLS and GMPLS Point to Point and Point to Multi-point Traffic Engineered LSPs.

In this architecture path computation does not necessarily occur on the head-end (ingress) LSR, but on some other path computation entity that may physically not be located on each head-end LSR.

From the charter it is apparent that this WG is focused on MPLS technologies, as opposed to the I2RS, which is focused on IP routing technologies. The SDN-like applicability comes from the notion that the path computation entity need not be physically located on the networking device itself (i.e., the MPLS head-end LSR), as is the case with all MPLS routers today. What is not obvious from the charter is that this is yet another example of a "hybrid network" model of SDN. The PCE WG is not trying to remove all of the MPLS control plane functionality from the networking devices themselves (i.e., the Path Computation Clients, or PCCs); but rather, the intent is to augment the distributed MPLS network domain with additional functionality that is very likely logically centralized in one or more PCEs. The PCE will have global knowledge of the MPLS domain (it even has applicability for inter-domain MPLS) and it will be able to make near real-time decisions in order to optimize the MPLS traffic engineering network. It will continue to leverage the RSVP-TE protocol that is widely deployed today, although enhancements to RSVP-TE may be required.

The I2RS is relatively new and no new protocols or mechanisms have yet been proposed by the WG. Therefore, the PCE activity is the prime WG within the IETF that has SDN-like applicability and that will initially pave the way forward for how existing networks will become SDN-enabled.

Border Gateway Protocol Link State (BGP-LS)

There is related work going on in the Inter-Domain Routing WG of the IETF. There is an Internet Draft, referred to as BGP-LS, that describes the capability to (once again) extend BGPv4 to include a new Network Layer Reachability Information (NLRI) encoding format. This NLRI would encode information from a network device's Traffic-Engineering Database (TED). The TED is built by OSPF or ISIS using TE extensions, and the TED is queried by RSVP-TE on each MPLS node to determine how to set up and/or optimize its LSPs. In currently deployed networks, each MPLS node maintains its own TED but now the TED can be exported from a route reflector to an external application. This external application can be a SDN application for global optimization, so there is the tie-in with "other things SDN."

BGP-LS only focuses on the mechanism to export the TED information and does not yet describe how SDN-like applications can use this information. However, one example is PCE; a logically centralized PCE could receive TED information from BGP-LS as input into its traffic-engineering optimization application. There could be other uses for exporting this type of information from a routed and/or MPLS network so the applicability of BGP-LS could become larger over time.

Service Function Chaining (SFC)

The SFC WG is another recent addition to the IETF that is closely related to SDN. This work was originally going to be done in a Network Service Chaining WG but that WG never materialized and the activity was moved into this new WG instead. The NSC was intended to be the host for service chaining standards, based on a recent IETF Birds of a Feather (BOF) on the applicability and need for a service chaining and a service insertion capability. All this work is now being done in the SFC WG.

Service chaining is a very old problem that has not yet had an efficient and scalable solution. The need to tie functions together in a service chain is now becoming even more problematic, with the degree of virtualization the various network functions are experiencing. Firewalls, load balancers, and even routers are being virtualized at a very rapid pace of innovation. Even for non-virtualized functions, there needs to be an ability to properly "steer" traffic to each of the network functions in order to insert the proper service into the data flow. This traffic steering requirement can be needed at a very granular level, even at the IP flow level. The legacy ways of meeting this requirement using VLANs or Policy-Based Routing (PBR) have never been optimal, scalable, dynamic, or efficient. Clearly a new method of meeting the requirement needs to be created.

One such method was described in Chapter 5. That method described the use the OpenFlow protocol to accomplish the very granular traffic steering capability required for dynamic, efficient service chaining. So, there is one tie-in to SDN, and the other is that the traffic steering/service chaining application could be an SDN application that resides on an SDN controller platform.

Other SFC solutions involve encapsulation overlays, which are also somewhat related to SDN in the SDDC context. It will be interesting to see which types of solutions ultimately evolve from the SFC WG and begin to gain acceptance into the marketplace. The Network Service Header (NSH) overlay is one solution that seems to be gaining early acceptance; however, its still a long way from standardization.

Network Virtualization Overlays (NVO3)

NVO3 was also previously discussed in this book, but it's worth mentioning again as part of this chapter. NVO3 focuses on the data center virtualization component that comprises a key piece of an overall Software Defined Data Center (SDDC) solution.

Since NVO3 was covered in detail in previous chapters, it won't also be explained here.

Forwarding and Control Element Separation (FORCES)

FORCES has been around the IETF since 2005; however, the activity has not been what one would describe as exciting until this new SDN paradigm took hold. FORCES describes a capability that is very similar to a purist ONF view of SDN (i.e., a clear physical separation of the control plane from the forwarding plane in networking devices). The activity and interest level in this WG has picked up somewhat now that it is being intentionally correlated to SDN.

While this work is interesting and is now being related to SDN, what is not clear is whether the protocols and technologies that come from this WG will ever be deployed in any meaningful way. Some of the activities, terminology, and mechanisms within FORCES are being adapted to be more friendly to current SDN solutions. While it is unclear whether FORCES will have a meaningful impact on the emerging SDN architecture, it is worth following because at a minimum, the many lessons that have been learned in the creation of the FORCES architecture can and should be leveraged in related and emerging SDN architectures and solutions.

Does NFV = SDN?

Network Function Virtualization (NFV) has taken quite a bit of buzz from SDN. What is amazing is that NFV as a network and architectural requirement has only recently emerged in a coherent fashion. The European Telecommunications Standards Institute (ETSI) is the current placeholder for all things NFV, but the concept and requirements were initially defined and documented in an industry "Call to Action" white paper crafted by many global service providers. This industry wide effort, or rather one could say it was a "demand," came from the many SPs who can no longer support the way that network and service functions are deployed in their networks. Today, these many network functions are deployed with stand-alone, proprietary and hardware-based appliances. That often equates to "high cost." These various appliances are made by many different vendors, so the SP not only has the burden of deploying and managing these many different appliances and devices, but it also must cope with the challenges of interoperability amongst these many devices. The current method of doing this raises serious questions as to the sustainability of building networks in this manner. The massive CAPEX and OPEX burdens are enormous and these costs must be brought down.

To solve this massive problem, it is necessary to virtualize the functionality of these many network and service functions and run this software on common and standard hardware; often referred to as Commercial Off The Shelf (COTS) hardware. This is the essence of the NFV movement. Please refer to the ETSI website below.

[http://www.etsi.org/news-events/news/700-2013-10-etsi-publishes-first-nfv-specifications]

Many NFV use cases are defined as part of this effort. They can be viewed here:

[http://www.etsi.org/deliver/etsi_gs/NFV/001_099/001/01.01.01_60/gs_NFV001v010101p.pdf]

While many of these use cases are clearly relevant to SPs, some of them seem to fall into a gray area. There are many Proof of Concepts (POC) and trials going on across the globe for deploying NFV functionality into networks. This is truly an innovative, architecture changing dynamic that is being witnessed with NFV. Many incumbent and new networking vendors are racing to offer to the market their version of a Virtualized Network Function (VNF).

So, back to the question at hand – does NFV = SDN?

NFV and SDN are two distinct yet very complementary models of networking. They are not equal to each other, but they are also not mutually exclusive. How and whether they work together will depend on the deployment model of how these new services and solutions are rolled-out into real networks. A network could deploy an SDN controller platform for the SDDC and NFV could be a primary component of the SDDC solution. Alternately, NFV could be deployed without the automation of an SDN controller platform. It is clear that NFV would benefit greatly from the automation and programmatic capabilities of a SDN controller platform; but again, it really depends on how these new solutions are deployed. Ultimately, it seems evident that they will be deployed together in a coherent and somewhat inclusive manner. They clearly benefit from each other in terms of offering an overall solution.

So, one way of looking at this is that NFV + SDN = SDDC. Having said that, NFV and SDN are not solely contained solutions that only apply to the data center. The wide area and campus networks will also benefit from NFV and SDN solutions.

One other thing worth noting with NFV (and SDN in general), is that while the service providers are currently the ones driving the industry to move towards a virtualized network function, once these solutions are available they will be deployed by other types of networks, including enterprise networks. The NFV movement will benefit networks of every type. Also worth following is how the networking vendor community evolves to provide these virtualized network functions. Some of these vendors will not embrace this movement as much as other vendors, out of fear of hardware sales cannibalization. The NFV movement will definitely disrupt the networking vendor apple cart!

Vendor Proprietary SDNs

Some networking vendors continue to build their own proprietary flavors of "SDN." This should not be much of a surprise at first thought, but in this day and age of open standards and open source, this does seem inconsistent to say the least. It is apparent to most of the folks involved in SDN that open source and open standards are the future. The entire SDN ecosystem is purposely being built on the "openness" mantra. Why would vendors continue the age old strategy of "vendor lock-in" with proprietary solutions? A rhetorical question, of course.

So, this section will be short since vendor proprietary SDN solutions are clearly not the norm, and as a result, their future deployment adoption is still questionable. Well, except for perhaps one particular solution.

VMware vCloud, vCenter, and NSX

vCloud is the premier cloud networking solution from VMware, for enterprises that desire to migrate their internal cloud to a remote cloud computing solution. The gotcha is that all the hypervisor and cloud computing systems must be based on VMware. So, this is a proprietary flavor of a cloud computing SDN solution.

vCenter is a centralized platform for managing a VMware data center environment. NSX is a virtual networking solution that combines aspects of VMware's vCloud networking and security offering with the acquired Nicira Networks Virtualization Platform (NVP). This is the primary SDN offering for the software-defined data center from VMware. It is also proprietary although there are aspects of NSX that could run on open systems, such as KVM.

One advantage that VMware has in this space is the leverage they have due to their large marketshare in virtualized servers. However, their overall "SDN-like" solution is considered a proprietary and closed one.

Cisco ACI

Cisco's recent offering, Application Centric Infrastructure (ACI), is an attempt to re-shape the SDN conversation into their vision of what and how an "SDN-like" solution should provide. It is clearly being positioned against the VMware solution and the open standards and open source solutions that are emerging in the market-place, such as OpenStack and OpenDaylight.

One significant difference in ACI, as opposed to NSX for example, is that the ACI architecture requires specific hardware devices to be deployed in the data center, and these networking devices must be from Cisco. So, it is yet another version of a proprietary "SDN-like" solution from a vendor (VMware being the other prime example), with the distinct differentiation of this being more of a hardware-defined networking solution rather than software-defined.

Speaking of Hardware Defined Networking

Open Compute Project (OCP)

Facebook started an open computing platform project a few years ago, called Open Compute Project (OCP). The goal is to "build one of the most efficient computing infrastructures at the lowest possible cost." The idea is to promote open computing platforms and specifications to develop servers and data centers, following the same type of open source model that has been shown successful in the software-defined networking space.

OCP now hosts an Open Compute Summit that has started to gain real momentum. Intel and Broadcom, among other silicon vendors, are showing genuine interest in publishing open compute and open switch platform specifications. While OCP began as an open source community for open computing platforms, open networking switch specifications are now being widely discussed and are being made available to the community. Open source is really changing the industry, not just in software, but now in hardware as well! Exciting times indeed.

Open Data Plane

A very recent addition to the open source hardware paradigm is the Open Data Plane organization.

[http://www.opendataplane.org/]

This is a very interesting community organization that intends to develop an open source, cross-platform set of APIs for the networking data plane. This is a true Hardware Defined Networking (HDN) community of open source developers.

Final Thoughts on Other Things SDN

My, we are in interesting times, are we not!? There are many things within the SDN context, including the important NFV movement. There are many things related to SDN as well, and we have discussed some of these in this chapter. What is important is that the networking industry is evolving very rapidly before our very eyes and one must keep an eye and ear to the various movements to remain relevant.

Some of these related movements will not survive this market transition we are currently experiencing. There will likely be additional movements that are not even mentioned here. One thing is certain – networking is no longer boring!

One can relate parts of this networking transition to the mainframe transition of the 1980s. Before the advent of the personal computer and its related disaggregated architecture, computers were closed and vertically integrated. A vendor offered the entire system in a closed and proprietary manner. Remember the IBM mainframe? And the DEC VAX? Those were closed systems, and a single vendor offered the complete package: the hardware, the operating system and the software applications. Then came the PC era and not only did the systems function on "common hardware," but the system itself became disaggregated. We could install one operating system on the hardware and then install a different supplier's software applications! Each component within the system became inter-changeable; the OS could even be replaced with a different one if the user so desired. Now, the networking industry is moving towards such a model. This is completely unprecedented and very exciting!

Summary

It is apparent that OpenFlow is not the only gig in town. There are a great deal of other solutions that all fit under the SDN + NFV umbrella. It seems every major networking vendor and certainly a good number of startup companies all have their own vision and utilize many different technologies to accomplish their goals. What is the best solution? Time will tell, but for now there are many options to select from when considering the best way to solve the business case for your organization.

8

Volume II: A Look Ahead

This final chapter will provide a short glimpse of what is being written for Volume II of this three-volume series on SDN.

Well, we've covered quite a bit of things in this volume already! As the authors intended, this book series is not attempting to "boil the ocean" when it comes to writing about SDN. There are too many topics and trends to discuss them all; and some of them are or will become irrelevant anyway. The focus of Volume I is on OpenFlow and how it relates to SDN. Many other topics were covered, but the intended focus is on OF.

Now you may ask ... what is in store for Volume II?

More Use Cases

Yes, we've heard your call! While a good portion of volume I covered various SDN use cases, Volume II will have many more. This is an area where most of the common questions come from when it comes to SDN: *"What problem does SDN really solve and when will it be available?"* This all comes down to the use case, and there are many of them in various stages of development, testing, and deployment.

We will continue our pattern of covering use cases and solutions that leverage the OF protocol, and those which do not. A few of the more interesting and relevant use cases that volume II will cover are:

1. Network Analytics
2. Traffic Engineering
3. Network Service Chaining and Service Function Chaining
4. Data Center Overlay Solutions
5. SDN in Mobile Networks
6. Network Function Virtualization and Virtual Network Functions

Data Center Underlay and Overlay Integration

Data center (DC) networks continue to undergo major transformational innovations, particularly as this volume is being written. We're in the midst of the most major DC transformation in a few decades. Networking is exciting again! One area that is touched on briefly in this volume but will be greatly expanded on in volume II is how the DC underlay and overlay networks integrate. Or do they? One may wonder whether the underlay and overlay should even become an integrated network; so, that is a nice starting point for further discussion in this area.

Industry Standards Bodies

Prominent industry standards bodies are covered in some degree of detail in Volume I; however, this is also an area that is evolving quite rapidly. As the DC network undergoes its transformation, multi-vendor and open standard protocols, mechanisms and solutions must come to market. Single vendor and proprietary solutions are no longer the choice for a large majority of network operators. Those days are now past us.

IETF Updates

Volume II will cover the IETF in more detail. It will cover the updates in the working groups that were already discussed as well as some of the newer activities. Some of the more prominent working groups that will be covered are:

1. NVO3
   1. The WG is currently re-chartering but will remain focused on standards for the DC overlay architecture.
2. PCE
3. SPRING
   1. New WG focused on non-shortest-path and source-routing in IP networks. May require a new packet header, or can leverage existing headers.

4. SFC
   1. New concepts for network service chaining headers are being defined. One example is the Network Service Header (NSH).
5. SDN RG
   1. Gaining tremendous interest in the Internet Research Task Force (IRTF).
6. NFV RG
   1. New IRTF WG being formed around NFV.
7. BESS
   1. Newly formed BGP Enabled Services WG.

ONF Updates

Similar to the IETF, the ONF and its various WGs continue to evolve and innovate in the SDN problem space. While the ONF is mostly focused on OpenFlow, they have also branched out into the more general SDN space as of late. Some of the more interesting activities in the ONF that will be updated include:

1. Forwarding Abstractions WG (FAWG)
   1. OpenFlow Table Type Patterns (TTPs)
2. Chip Advisory Board (CAB)
3. Northbound Interface WG (NBI)

Open Source Updates

Open source is the *call to action* for many of today's innovations! Enough said.

Open Daylight

Open Daylight released the Hydrogen platform in early 2014. The current release is Helium and it will be covered in detail in Volume II. The ODL platform continues to gain wide industry acceptance and is in the early stages of testing and deployment. It is expected to become the industry's "de-facto" SDN controller platform. The exciting progress and deployment models will be discussed.

Open Stack

Similar to ODL, the OpenStack community continues to innovate; however, it is primarily focused on DC orchestration. The many updates and deployments of OpenStack will be included.

Open Daylight + Open Stack

We only briefly mentioned this area briefly in this volume but we will expand upon it in the next volume: how do ODL and OS coexist and/or integrate into the same network environment? How is the work split between the two platforms? Which APIs will be needed? Is it a North/South or East/West integration model? Early thinking has this as a North/South API model. This is an early area of activity and there is not a lot of detail available in this area as of this writing. Volume II will contain many details of this evolving project.

Open Compute Project

The OCP appears to be gaining industry and community traction, particularly as it evolves to include the DC network switch infrastructure and not just the compute side of the DC. While the original community effort of OCP was focused solely on openness and disaggregation of server hardware and software, the community is now moving this model into the DC network switch infrastructure.

One example of this is the announcement of the Facebook "Wedge" and "FBOSS" efforts. In addition to that, chip vendors such as Broadcom and Intel are rapidly moving into the network switching marketplace with efforts such as Red Rock Canyon from Intel and all the work that Broadcom is doing with the Trident chipsets.

Open Networking User Group

Unlike the other open groups listed in this section, the Open Networking User Group (ONUG) does not create standards or specify technologies. Instead, ONUG is dedicated to sharing experience among open networking technology. Their conferences are made up solely of IT executives and industry analysts: vendors and reporters are not invited to speak.

Relevant to this book, ONUG is a strong advocate of SDN and network programmability. Speakers at ONUG events share their experiences and provide lessons learned to the user group.

More OpenFlow

As expected, all the continued innovations in OpenFlow will be covered in detail! One example is the recently released OF v1.5 spec that is currently being reviewed.

Network Function Virtualization!

Much like OF was the focus topic in Volume I, NFV will be the primary focus topic in Volume II.

The NFV movement is moving along at an accelerated pace. It's hard to believe that this industry movement was really only started in 2013 with the publication of the service provider white paper and *call to action*. Many NFV related use cases are now being documented and are in early stages of development and Proof-of-Concept (POC) testing.

While some people like to distinguish between NFV and SDN, they are very complementary industry movements and will very likely be deployed in unison. They are not mutually inclusive however, so they are evolving at independent rates.

Open NFV

Recently organized Open NFV (OPNFV) will be covered in detail in Volume II.

ETSI Updates

While ETSI could have been mentioned earlier in this chapter, under the Industry Standards section, it is more appropriate to include it here under NFV. ETSI continues to influence the NFV movements and has recently been granted a two-year extension.

Other things SDN

This list of topics is not comprehensive. As rapid innovations continue in software-defined and software-driven networking, many other activities and solutions will come to market and they will be covered as well.

See you in Volume II!